To Mikeing?
Happy reading!
With love —
Betty

1982

WALK
WITH GOD
BETWEEN
SUNDAYS

WALK
WITH GOD
BETWEEN SUNDAYS

Richard C.
Halverson

Ronald N. Haynes Publishers, Inc.
P.O. BOX 2748 / PALM SPRINGS, CALIFORNIA

WALK WITH GOD BETWEEN SUNDAYS

Copyright © 1981 by Richard C. Halverson
Library of Congress Catalog Card Number 81-83842

ISBN: 0-88021-034-6
Manufactured in the United States of America
Published by Ronald Haynes Publishers, Inc.
Palm Springs, California 92263

To
Abraham Vereide
whose dedication to Christ issued a passion
for a "leadership led by God." His mission:
to inspire men to live Christ around the clock
seven days a week wherever they are,
whatever they do.

CONTENTS

WALK WITH GOD BETWEEN SUNDAYS

§ *BETWEEN SUNDAYS*

*C*hristianity is made for the road not the sanctuary!
Christianity took root where the only sanctuary was a Jewish temple or synagogue, and very soon the Church was driven from both. For three centuries Christian faith was propagated in homes and market places, prisons and catacombs.

Even with the coming of the great cathedrals and through the medieval period, fellowship continued in the home and the market place. Worship happened whenever Christians were able to meet, under whatever circumstances, wherever they were. The chance meeting of two Christians unexpectedly would be the occasion for expressions of love and loyalty to Christ, reminiscing, discussion of apostles' teaching and prayer. Under intimidation and persecution Christians sought each other under pain of death, shared faith and nourished one another in fellowship.

The sanctuary is a fact of contemporary Christianity which is probably here to stay, but the caricature of worship is the idea that it is limited to a special place at a particular time in a peculiar way, and usually dependent upon a "professional" for leadership.

"Sanctuaryism" has isolated Christianity from life. Church now means the building; and the average American, Christian or otherwise, consciously or unconsciously relates Christian faith to what goes on inside the building at certain stated times in certain technical ways. And he fails to see any connection between that and what goes on downtown Monday through Saturday.

Lost is the spontaneity of primitive Christian worship, and with it, more often than not, the power and relevance of faith to life.

Authentic Christianity is a life to be lived midst the hard facts of history. It is designed for the home and community, the office and the shop, the club and the campus, the market, factory and farm! Christianity is for every day, wherever one is, under whatever circumstances. Sunday may remain peculiarly devoted to the sanctuary, but worship and practice should never be limited to this.

Christianity is for *between Sundays*!

"Again I say to you, if two of you agree on earth about anything they ask, it will be done for them by My Father in Heaven. For where two or three are gathered in My Name, there am I in the midst of them" (Matthew 18:19, 20).

§ TO BE A MAN IS TO BE GODLIKE

Man was made "in the image of God...." Obviously the more Godlike a man is the more manlike he will be! And conversely, the less like God he is the less of a man he is!

One of the most insidious, diabolical lies ever perpetrated on humanity is the insinuation that Godlikeness means shallow, prudish, blue-nosed piety. Jesus was perfect, Godlike, and He was a Man of men, a Man in the fullest sense of the word...perfect Man. In fact, He was the only "normal" Man who ever lived. Man out of touch with God is subnormal.

Jesus Christ was normal, but He was not pious in the accepted sense of that word today. On the contrary. He upset all the concepts of piety held by His contemporaries. He was continually breaking their pious, religious codes. To the religionists of His day, Jesus was highly irreligious! They labeled Him "a drunkard, a glutton, a wine bibber." He drew His greatest hostility from the most religious.

In the strictest sense of the word, the grace of God works in a man to make him more Christlike. It might be said that the goal of the Heavenly Father in the life of the Christian is to make him like His Son. As the process of becoming more like the Son of God develops in a man he grows in manliness—he becomes more and more the man God intended. This is basic: the more like Christ a man is the more manly he will be; the less Christlike, the less of a man!

The measure of manhood is the measure of a man's Godliness. As God created man originally, only God can fashion manhood. It takes God to make a man! Wise therefore the man who consents to the Father's will, who yields to the daily ministry of the Holy Spirit in conforming him into the image of God's perfect Son.

"We all, with unveiled face, beholding the glory of the Lord, are being changed into His likeness..." (II Corinthians 3:18).

§ *MAN POWER*

*G*od's method is men! When He has a job to do, He seeks an available man through whom to work. Just as Jesus Christ entered history to do the Father's will (Hebrews 10:5-8), so He expects His disciples to do the Father's will. This in fact is man's glory—man's fulfillment —man's perfection. Man living for the glory of God is man as he was intended; man committed to anything less is a caricature.

The basic impact of the Church in history is not institutional or monolithic; it is not the resolutions and declarations of Councils or Boards important as they are; nor is it the influence of the "professionals," the clergy, the missionaries, the evangelists, essential though they be. The cutting edge of the Church on the world is the aggregate of the individual influence of millions of faithful Christians in their day-to-day living.

Christ has His men everywhere! He has placed them where they are. The "salt of the earth" and "light of the world," they have infiltrated, penetrated every segment of society; redemptive agents of love and light and power, they encircle the earth rubbing elbows with all humanity from royalty to rabble. They are of every color, race and language. They are in parliaments and palaces, factories and farms, markets and mills, campuses and clubs. They are in labor, business, industry, science, education and the professions. They preside over governments, practice law and medicine and dentistry; they dig ditches, raise sheep, hogs, cattle and grain; they dig in mines and manage giant corporations; they teach, do scientific and technological research, pilot aircraft and create music, literature and art. Christ's men are everywhere doing everything! And wherever he is, whatever he is doing, the true Christian is Christ's servant committed to His will.

There are approximately one billion nominal Christians in the world, one person out of three. Think of the incalculable impact on sin and secularism if every one of those so-called Christians were really committed to Christ and living it out daily. Academic to be sure, but this is not. You and I are somewhere right now, doing something. Are you—am I living for Christ here and now? Authentic Christian influence begins right where we are, right now!

Our hope for spiritual refreshing does not lie in the debut of some powerful preacher. It waits for the serious dedication of those men who profess faith in Christ but live as though it doesn't matter.

"Ye are my witnesses…!"

§ CHRISTIAN INFLUENCE

*T*alk about infiltration! Communism can't hold a candle to this! Christ has His men everywhere!

Real impact of the Church is not some huge religious combine, power bloc or pressure group, overpowering by sheer force of numbers… not a massive show of solidarity or organizational might. The power of Christ's Church is infinitely more subtle, infinitely more effective! The significance of man's Intelligence and Counter-intelligence work is infinitesimal compared to God's infusion of Christians into all of life everywhere.

The Divine strategy is the Christian man, at his job day in day out, bearing witness to Christ by life and lip right where he lives and works. In business and industry, the government and professions, labor, education, the military...in strategic places around the world: behind the iron curtain, probably right in the Kremlin and Peking. (He had men in Caesar's household in Paul's day.)

This spiritual penetration is the clue to the incredible, incalculable impact of Christianity worldwide! The Christian teacher doing his job to the glory of God, not preaching, just living Christ around the clock, honoring Christ in his daily walk and talk. The student witnessing for Christ on the campus: in fraternity house or dormitory, on the football field, in the student lounge. The Christian labor leader, businessman, military officer, policeman, surgeon, dentist, architect, groceryman, contractor, homemaker, barber, automobile dealer, farmer, lawyer, accountant. Those in Congress and parliaments, in the Pentagon and the State Department, in banks and clubs and lodges, in coal mines and steel mills, et cetera.

Multiply these by a million—by ten million—by a hundred million, and you have the true picture of Christian influence...invincible Christianity! Each Christian in his God-directed place, doing his job for God's glory, faithful to his church, strengthened by daily Bible study and prayer, saying a word for Christ as opportunity affords. Making his little world a better place by being there, like a benevolent infection, spiritually contagious. Like salt making life savory; like light shining in a dark place.

Christ is Lord! Nothing is more certain than that He will triumph— is triumphing in history. The decisive blow was the cross—the Resurrection. His redeemed ones are everywhere, the "savour of life unto life and death unto death."

§ ONE MAN—AND GOD

*G*od's method is men, not machinery! When God wants to get a thing done He seeks out a man; He does not build an organization. There is no limit to what God can do when He gets a man really dedicated to Himself. And by the same token there is no limit to the way machinery can bog down God's program when it gets the upper hand. Begin in Genesis and go through the Bible. You will discover that it is the story of men in the hands of God. You can hang every important event in the Bible on the life of one man thoroughly "sold out" to God.

Personality is the most precious commodity in the world. There is nothing that compares with it. It is the most powerful, too. Far more powerful than machines or organizations. In God's scheme, everything is subservient to personality. Go against that: trouble comes. In management-labor relations for example, treat labor like chattel—impersonally, en masse—you only aggravate the problem. God never intended man to be subordinated to machinery. That is why Communism cannot work in the last analysis: because the system becomes more important than the individuals who comprise it. It holds the seeds of its own destruction. Hitler could not make it work, nor Stalin. Neither could Khrushchev, nor can his successors!

Neither can some short-sighted managers. Bend personality into a mold. It just will not stay. There is more to the labor problem than raising pay and creating better working conditions. Especially when you do it in the same way that you overhaul machinery: clean it, oil it. There is something infinitely more important! Recognize the man himself—his personality, desires, his ego. That is the key to the whole business. Give a man his "place under the sun," recognize him as a man, and he will burn himself out to produce for you. Frustrate personality, and he will smolder until he explodes.

There is not an industry in the world that is worth as much, by God's standards, as any single individual working in it. "What shall it profit a man if he gain the whole world and lose his own soul?" Dwight L. Moody, while still a shoe salesman, heard a preacher say: "The world has yet to see what God can do with one man who is absolutely consecrated to Him." Moody determined to be that man. He moved two continents for God! You cannot estimate what God would do with you —through you, if you really took Him seriously, gave yourself to Him. Dedicate yourself to God, completely, and it will amaze you what He will do with you—for you—through you!

"I beseech you therefore, brethren, by the mercies of God, that you present your bodies a living sacrifice, wholly acceptable to God, which is your reasonable service" (Romans 12:1).

§ GOD'S METHOD

*O*ne man and God always make a *majority*!

God's method is men. If God can find a man who is available, willing, committed, there is *no limit* to what He can do through him! Some of the greatest exploits of history are the stories of one man—and *God*! (Think of the institutions, the organizations, the movements that are dominated by Godless men followed by the masses. Most people like to follow; and if there is not a Godly man to follow, they will follow a Godless one.)

Four of the saddest words ever penned are found in Ezekiel's prophecy. Israel had forsaken God, had forgotten her former ways. Her life was filled with lewdness, idolatry and abominable practices. Then Ezekiel says God sought for a man among them, just *one man* who would obey God and take the place of leadership for *Him*. Then come these pathetic words: *"But I found none!"* Not even *one* man among them who was willing to turn from his wickedness, his slothfulness, his selfishness, his apathy and indolence. Not one man who was willing to *obey* God, to take a stand for righteousness!

It brings to mind a recent experience with a fraternity president. A minister went to him asking if there would be any possibility of meeting with the house to present the Christian message apart from any sectarian touch. As they talked the college man broke into tears. "I've been hoping something like this would happen," he said. "This house is *going to hell* and I haven't known what to do about it!" The minister was invited back. The response to his message was astounding! This led to a movement that has now reached into hundreds of fraternity and sorority houses on scores of campuses all over the country. Thousands of students have heard the message.

All God needed was *one* man in a fraternity house. That is all God needs anywhere—no matter what the conditions! If God can find one man who will follow, there is no limit to what *He* can do! This is the New Testament method! Men committed to Jesus Christ, penetrating their society for Him. *Laymen* reaching into places where a minister cannot go; or if he can, he will not be accepted.

It was never the Lord's intention that the priceless message of the Gospel should be the exclusive property of professional clergy. On the contrary. *Every* Christian was commissioned to witness—to tell the good news! There are lots of little worlds: societies, crowds, institutions, going to hell today for want of *one man* who will stand in the gap, take Christ seriously, who will obey God! All God needs is *you*! How about it?

§ *DISTRIBUTION*

*I*n the field of economics it is not a matter of supply nor of demand that is the basic problem. It is a matter of distribution. There is certainly no doubt about demand! The world is full of it: millions, literally millions, in China, India, Korea, starving. Not to mention Europe, Britain, and even the United States. Nor is it a question of supply! The plain fact is our granaries are glutted with over-supplies. We have even resorted to the destruction of enormous food wealth as artificial means of leveling off supply. Furthermore, whenever a man is helped to be productive, his need is met and he increases supply. It is, however, maladjustment to meet a man's need without making him productive. That is the insidious evil in socialism.

The fundamental problem is how to bring the abundant supply and demand together: how to bridge the chasm between resources and need. Distribution is the solution. It is the big economic problem in the world today. The tragedy is that men are trying to solve it artificially, in complete disregard of economic law. Some day we shall pay through the nose for the sinful destruction of food products, or for deliberate non-production. These are utterly false economics!

But the point is that the same law applies in the spiritual realm. The spiritual problem is not one of supply or demand, it is one of distribution. No one would question the need for spirituality today. From every source: military, political, educational, scientific, the cry is for spiritual resources as the only "out"—the only cure for our headlong plunge to chaos. Nor can the supply be doubted. For in Christ we have an unlimited supply of spiritual resources. God's grace is inexhaustible. You can't run out of it! You can't use it up. There is no end to God's resources.

Question is one of distribution. How to get God's resources over against the needs of men. Key to this is the Christian man! Because in the economy of God it is His plan that Divine resources flow through the Christian. Every Christian ought to be a channel for God's blessing. The only way the grace of God can be directed to the needy field: home, office, plant, neighborhood, community—is to flow through consecrated Christians. It means that you yourself, right where you are, must be a means of distribution! Close your heart, refuse to yield completely to Christ as a channel of blessing, and you shut off the flow of God's grace to that area of life you touch. It is entirely up to you! Either you are a channel—or a dam! That is the reason why your consecration is imperative, *if you are a Christian!*

"Now unto Him that is able to do exceedingly abundantly above all that we ask or think, according to the power that worketh in us..." (Ephesians 3:20).

§ *DISCIPLESHIP IS NOW—HERE!*

*D*iscipleship begins right where you are! A man becomes restless—casts a covetous glance in some other direction toward some other man who seems to be more successful, who seems more satisfied, more useful, happier. With envy he wishes he could be in the other fellow's place. "The grass is always greener in the other fellow's yard." Until you get over there! If the situation were reversed, the other man would still seem the satisfied, successful, happy one. This is the illusion of immaturity!

Geographic change does not make an effective man, nor do circumstances. If a man is not doing a good job for Christ where he is, he will probably not do a good job for Christ wherever he goes. There are certain exceptions to be sure, but—geography is no cure for poor discipleship! "Never allow the thought 'I am of no use where I am.' You certainly are of no use where you are not" (Oswald Chambers). Because the change does not need to come in the man's circumstances, the change needs to come first in the man himself! *Right where he is!* This is where effective discipleship begins—though it may not end here.

A man may be in the wrong place but the way to find it out is not to experiment by moving. The way to find out is to commit himself to Christ where he is—commit his circumstances to Christ as they are—then allow God to initiate whatever change may be in line with His will. When a man is dissatisfied the temptation will usually be to make a change, losing sight of the fact that God may cause (or allow) a restless spirit to overtake him because God wants to sharpen that man, lead him into new spiritual depths, increase his effectiveness. Restlessness is often the antidote for apathy. If a man moves instead of committing, he misses the blessing and will likely discover he belongs where he was in the first place. And often the first change is the beginning of a chain reaction that leads to change after change and produces a spiritual tramp who never settles down.

An interesting incident in the life of the Lord illustrates this. He came upon His disciples mending their nets on the beach following a night of fruitless toil. After speaking with them He admonished, "Let down your nets into the deep...." "But Lord," they said, "we have toiled all night and caught nothing. Nevertheless *at thy word* we shall...." They did. And they made such a great catch their boats could not hold it and their nets broke with the load.

Obedience turned failure into success—fruitless toil into productivity! The secret was commitment right where they were, where they had toiled all night and caught nothing, right at the scene of their failure. Begin where you are to give yourself to Jesus Christ in whatever circumstances. Obey Him at that point. He will make the changes that ought to come.

"Commit thy way unto the Lord, trust also in Him, and *He shall bring it to pass*" (Psalm 37:5).

§ COME! GO!

*H*ealthy Christianity is elliptical. It polarizes around two opposing, harmonious forces. One is centripetal: the invitation, "Come." The other is centrifugal: the commission, "Go!" Either without the other produces the eccentric. Together they put the Christian in orbit.

Jesus said, "Come unto Me...." The Christian life begins with this— a sincere response to His gentle, firm invitation. But that is just the beginning. A man must know Jesus to serve Him. He must come to Jesus to know Him. Coming to Jesus qualifies a man to go to others, but until a man comes to Jesus, his going is useless and purposeless. Coming to Jesus resolves the sin-guilt problem. Guilt is like sand in the human machinery. Until that is settled, friction increases and life grinds to a halt and burns out. Lots of heat and pressure, but no power.

Jesus is the "Lamb of God that taketh away the sin...." The oil of God's grace in Christ breaks the sin deadlock and frees the man. With sin forgiven and cleansed the regenerate man is ready to go in service. Jesus insisted upon this first: "Ye must be born again."

Then comes the commission: "Go into all the world bearing witness unto Me." Having received new life in Christ, take it to others. But until you have received it, you have nothing to give when you go!

Some men are always coming—never going anywhere. Spiritual sops, they are dominated by finicky spiritual appetites, constantly feeling their spiritual pulses—busy keeping score on themselves—preoccupied with the condition of their own piety. They are like spiritual hypochondriacs.

Some are just busy going. Theirs is the religion of the "do-gooder."

They are busy-bodies, generally in the way—a nuisance, playing amateur providence with others' lives, interfering, managing their friends. They are spiritual vacuums!

But the man who comes to Jesus and abides in Him, and then goes in His strength and love to others is a blessing to everyone within his orbit. His life, filled with the resources of Christ, is constantly channeling those resources to others.

"He who abides in Me, and I in him, he it is that bears much fruit" (John 15:5).

§ ALL YOURS!

*T*here is something new under the sun...and it's yours for the taking! Today is utterly new, untouched by human hands. You have as much time as the President of the United States or head of our largest corporation...and you probably have much less responsibility. The busiest man in the world is not granted a second more to do his job than you have to do yours! You've got as big a piece of time as any man alive!

But remember, you get it a minute at a time. You can't store it up and save it for later. Let a minute slip by; you've lost it forever. Time is irretrievable. You must use it as you get it, a minute at a time. Only way to save time is to spend it wisely. You can't hoard it and collect interest. You can't redeem it when it has gone. Either you spend it...or you lose it!

We can learn some things from Joshua, the sixth book in the Old Testament. Joshua is the book of new things: beginnings. Not just beginning from scratch either. Israel had been going in circles for forty years; now she is about to hit "pay dirt." Joshua is the record of this triumph from wilderness wandering to the land of milk and honey—from frustration to fulfillment. Joshua is the thrilling story of Israel's take-over in Canaan. The key: "Possess your possessions!" The new land had been waiting for forty years. It was all there. But it didn't "belong" to Israel until she took it. God had given it, but she didn't have the gift until she possessed it.

Today is yours—God's incalculable gift. Take it!

"Ye have not passed this way before" (Joshua 3:4). No matter how much the past has been messed up, this is new. No one's been over the ground. Past failures need not be carried over: God's grace in Christ tends to that!

"Every place that the sole of your foot shall tread upon, that have I given unto you" (1:3). Note God has already given it. You get it by taking it. Stake your claim. It's yours!

The secret for success is recorded in Joshua 1:9.

§ *WAY UNKNOWN? FUTURE SURE!*

*W*ho but a fool would set out on an unknown way without a navigator? Even the common tourist consults a road map! The dependable pilot does not "fly by the seat of his pants." He reckons on his instruments.

How then does the perceptive man approach the big unknown—the future? There are predictables, reasonably clear to a man of foresight—prophetic insights which no thoughtful man disregards. But by and large the future is a great unknown. For that matter so is tomorrow, or the next sixty minutes. Man is forever moving into the unknown. "You have not passed this way before," said the Lord to Joshua.

Sure life has continuity; and with a degree of reasonableness a man can know what lies ahead in the light of what's gone before. But what a catastrophe? Life is contiguous. It is also catastrophic! Discontinuity is also a fact! Gaps and contingencies make the future unknowable.

However, this does not mean that a man must face the future without a navigator, without direction, without guidance. On the contrary. That God takes a personal, detailed, intimate interest in the man who takes Him seriously is one of the most obvious truths in the Bible. God, who knows "the end from the beginning," who is the author of the future, will personally direct the steps of him who desires to be so led.

Abraham went out "not knowing whither he went." But he knew God! He did not know the way, but Abraham knew his Guide!

Daily thousands of men board airliners, entrusting their way to those who are qualified to transport them safely to their destination. How much more ought a man trust his way to the God who never fails! The future is not predictable, but God's faithfulness is! He can be known, understood, followed. He has made Himself known in Christ. His way is clear in Christ. Know Christ, know God! Follow Christ, follow God! Go with Christ! He is never taken by surprise— never overwhelmed by the unexpected. Christ knows the way.

"Commit thy way unto the Lord, trust also in Him, and He shall bring it to pass" (Psalm 37:5).

§ FAITH? IN WHAT?

*I*n the final analysis, you've got to believe somebody...even if that somebody is yourself alone. Some kind of a faith is inescapable.

Either you believe in God or you believe in no-god. If you believe in God, either you believe in the God of the Bible or some other. If you believe in some other god, then you believe that the Bible is untrustworthy. If you believe the Bible is untrustworthy, you must have some basis for such a belief. What is it? Who or what do you believe strongly enough to allow you to put aside the Bible?

Will the foundation of your belief stand the test of reality? The eternal welfare of your soul rides on this! Either you trust Jesus Christ, His Word and His work—or you do not! If you do not, on whom or what rests your eternal destiny?

Perhaps you do not believe in immortality. Very well, what is the ground for this belief? Where did you get it? Is your source trustworthy? Is it intelligent to risk your future with this source?

Is the foundation of your belief reliable enough to justify your rejection of Jesus Christ and His gift of eternal life? If the basis of your "faith" against Jesus and immortality is rational, is it dependable? To put it another way, do you have a reasonable faith or just opinions?

Assuming there is a risk in believing the Bible, in trusting Jesus Christ, is there a lesser risk in your belief? Where does the greater risk lie: In trusting Jesus, or something else—some*one* else? What person in history more merits your confidence? Who else than Jesus has so earned the right to be trusted by you?

You have a faith! Is it based on fact…or fancy?

"He that hears My words and doeth them not is like a man who builds his house on the earth and the floods beat against it vehemently and it falls; and great is its ruin!" (Luke 6:49).

§ *CONSIDER HIM!*

*C*onsider the greatest Man who ever lived! So many people have made up their minds about Jesus Christ on the basis of second-hand information. Take a minute to think straight about Him!

His is an historical figure. One bearing the name of Jesus Christ actually lived and worked and taught in a little country bordering the Mediterranean. History is divided by His life into B.C. and A.D. Every time you date a letter or use the calendar you acknowledge Him. He is the dividing point of history—the center of time. Charles Malik of Lebanon calls Him "the hinge of history."

His teaching was revolutionary. "Never man spake like this man!" His teaching is the highest known to man: His ethics are basic for life. He spoke with absolute authority on every subject. His life was exemplary. He was the epitome of virtue. It is impossible to think of a virtue that was not personified in His life. All goodness and greatness converged in His matchless Person. He suffered the injustice of an ignominious trial—the humiliation of a cruel death on a cross.

Three days after they put His body in a tomb, sealed it with a Roman seal, and stationed a platoon of soldiers about it, the seal was broken —the body gone! According to the testimony of more than five hundred people He was seen on many occasions for forty days following this event.

Men everywhere agree as touching the greatness of Jesus Christ—
His life and teachings. Yet men everywhere stubbornly ignore Him
and reject Him, blaspheme His Name in their daily conversation.
Why?

He claimed to be God. He did not say He was like God or a Prophet
of God, *but He said He was God*. He said to reject Him was to reject God
the Father. He said to dishonor Him was to dishonor God. He said
that obedience to His teaching constituted the only sure foundation
to life: that to disobey Him was like building your house on sand, and
to obey Him was like a wise man who built his house on a rock. He said
that men who did not believe on Him would die in their sins...that a
man's eternal destiny depended on his response to Christ. "He that
believeth not on Me is condemned already *because He has not believed....!*"

He said He was going to rise from the dead—that His Resurrection
would be the supreme sign that He was what He claimed to be: very
God of very God! His Resurrection is one of the most solidly established facts in history!

Jesus Christ is not a dead hero according to the testimony of millions. He is a contemporary Savior and Lord. He is alive—present
with all who will turn to Him—relevant to every need and issue of
life. Really now: what do you think of Christ? Is He just a name you
use to swear with? Or is He the Peerless Son of God, your Savior, your
Lord?

§ *WHEN IS A HERO?*

*C*ircumstances may not make the man, but they reveal him. Before
the crisis, the "hero" was just an "ordinary" man. The "stuff" of
the hero was in him; unusual circumstances brought it out. He didn't
wait for a crisis. He stuck to his job day in, day out, and was "Johnny
on the spot" when the crisis broke. As he functioned in the ordinary
situation, he functioned in a crisis!

Take Lincoln for example: lanky, ungainly, homely, poorly
dressed; and he had failed many times in politics. But he was God's

man for the crisis. He was "ripe" for his times, and the crisis revealed the man, galvanized his hidden resources into positive, constructive, successful action.

Not the man who makes things happen, but the one who is ready whatever happens—he it is who makes history. Under other circumstances George Washington could have been simply a successful farmer, living quietly on his Mt. Vernon acres. The greatness was there, but it took a Revolutionary War to bring it out.

Greatness is not something to be sought as an end in itself. The man who is ambitious to be great will probably never achieve greatness. Preoccupied with the distant dream, he neglects the present opportunity. Whereas the man who is doing the job in the present circumstances can be depended upon to do the job in the future crisis. Faithful here and now, he will be faithful there and then! Faithful in little things, he will be faithful in big ones.

The man who keeps waiting for the *big* chance never recognizes it when it comes. Downgrading the ordinary day-to-day affairs conditions him for failure in extraordinary times. If a man is not great when it doesn't matter, he will not be when it does! "It is required in stewards that a man be found faithful," admonished the Apostle Paul (I Corinthians 4:2).

Jesus said, "Well done good and faithful servant, you have been faithful over a little, I will set you over much" (Matthew 25:21 [RSV]).

§   *KNOW GOD*

*T*here's only one way really to know a person. That is to meet him first-hand. No matter how much you are told about a man, you never know him until you meet the man himself. It's possible to know all the data about the man: height, weight, build, color of hair, eyes, personality traits, distinguishing marks...and still miss him entirely when you pass him on the street. There's only one way really to know the man himself. That is to meet him face to face, spend time with him, cultivate him.

God is no exception to this! It is not enough to be told about Him, to have all the facts available. A theology is not enough! To know the facts about God is not enough! That is not reality. On the contrary it can be the worst kind of unreality! God may be a total stranger, even when a man has a head full of knowledge about Him. Belief in a creed, no matter how solid, how orthodox, how sound, can be the most intolerable, heartless, cold, unreasonable thing...without a first-hand acquaintance with Him who is behind the creed. Belief just in creed, belief just in facts about God, engenders a false kind of bumptious, ruthless, intolerant, callous security. Faith in God Himself engenders humbleness, understanding, deep certainty and love.

My first glimpse of the Rocky Mountains and the Pacific Ocean was breathless and overwhelming. Having been born and reared in North Dakota, mountains and ocean were a new experience at the age of nineteen. I had seen pictures of them and had heard them described by others who had seen them, but when I saw them for myself, nothing anyone had said about them compared with that first-hand experience. They simply beggared description.

That is the glorious, unspeakable, down-to-earth realism of the Christian faith. In the Person of Jesus Christ God can be known first-hand. Not a conjecture, not theoretically, not hypothetically, but experientially, intimately, personally. You can know the Lord as a daily reality in your life! You can enjoy the exquisite privilege of walking daily with God, not as an idea but as a fact—a living reality—if you open your heart to Christ.

"God was in Christ reconciling the world unto Himself" (II Corinthians 5:19). Jesus said, "If a man love Me, he will keep My words: and My Father will love him, and We will come unto him, and make Our abode with him" (John 14:23).

§ *NEW MAN*

*N*o matter how you look at it, following Jesus is a winning proposition! You simply can't lose. Obeying Him is life at its best! Because the Christian life works right now! It takes effect the moment a man believes—opens his heart to Christ—receives Him as Savior and Lord of his life.

Even if God had not given the wonderful promise of life after death, even if He had not guaranteed my eternal welfare and if what Christ could do for me were only in this life, it would still be wise to follow Him. Because following Jesus Christ pays off in this life! Not in a superficial, weak, parasitical sense. Not in the do-nothing-and-get-paid-for-it sense. Not in the sense of welfarism or statism nor some other cheap brand of "dole." But in the strong, manly sense. In the fact that Christ gives strength for every emergency of life. His grace, wisdom, strength are always available in time of need. Eternal life is now. It means quality of life, not just quantity, not just life in terms of length of years.

Christianity is not escapism! It does not eliminate life's problems, times of testing, periods of trial. It does mean that He is with me in the time of need. He is a "very present help in trouble." The problems don't change, but I do. I'm no longer overcome by them. I'm an overcomer! Because Christ makes any man a better man when He runs his life. He's a freer man, more efficient, stronger. Whatever a man can do without Christ, He can do infinitely better with Christ! This is the heart of the Gospel. That Jesus Christ makes a man over from the inside out, makes him a new man on the inside where it really matters. Quickens the man. Regenerates him. Energizes him with a new power in his life altogether.

This is what makes Christianity basic. It equips a man to live life to his outside best. It qualifies him for any situation he faces. When a man lets Jesus Christ into his life, all the power of Christ is available. And the power of Christ is the power of God—all sufficient—all the time! We're missing a big bet when we overlook the change God can work in our lives by the power of the Gospel. We're taking life's second, or third, or tenth best. We're selling ourselves down the river when we refuse to take Christ into our hearts—turn our lives over to Him. Give Him control!

"If any man be in Christ, he is a new creature: old things are passed away; behold all things are become new" (II Corinthians 5:17).

§ *TRUE FREEDOM*

*F*reedom is a great word! It's the heart of the authentic American way.

But we're losing it. We're losing it because we've lost its secret. We've made freedom something else than it was meant to be. It has come to mean "I can do as I please." That is not freedom; that is license! It is as un-American as Karl Marx. Doing as one pleases is utterly destructive of freedom. It leads inevitably, irrevocably, inexorably to bondage.

Freedom's delicate balance is the responsibility of the free. Every freedom has its contingent obligation. Neglect the obligation and you forsake the freedom. Freedom of life carries with it the obligation to protect life. It does not mean freedom to take life. It does not mean one can interfere with another's life. It does mean "I'm my brother's keeper." Freedom of speech does not give one the right to abuse speech. It does not mean a man can say or write anything he wants without regard for others. It is not freedom to lie, or to bear false witness, or to gossip. It is not even the freedom to tell the truth about others just because it's true. It does mean speech is to be used to protect the right of speech.

Freedom of worship, by the same token, does not mean freedom not to worship! This does not mean worship must be legislated: that men must be made to worship contrary to their own conscience and will. But it does mean that men who will not worship in the name of freedom of worship are forfeiting their right to such a freedom, not by any legal process, but by the law of God.

For men can be truly free only in an atmosphere which takes God seriously. The delicate plant of freedom prospers only in the soil of devout and Godly men. Secularism, like crab grass, chokes the life out of freedom. You don't have to be a student of history to prove this for yourself. The very men, who in the name of freedom, are trying to secularize our public life, are poisoning the roots which give them their freedom.

"The Lord knoweth the way of the righteous: but the way of the ungodly shall perish" (Psalm 1:6).

§ LIVE AND LET LIVE

"*L*ive and let live."
   A great philosophy of life...or is it?

That depends of course on precisely what a man means when he says it. It may be just another way of rationalizing oneself out of responsibility. Maybe it means "You leave me alone, and I'll leave you alone." "You let me do as I please, and I'll let you do as you please."

This friendly-sounding, pious little platitude may mean nothing more than "Get off my back!" It may be a hypocritical facade for negligence and selfishness—a cover-up for one's abdication from his obligations to others—a transparent effort to justify one's "I-can't-be-bothered" attitude. On the lips of some it is a lame excuse for sheer anarchy. As such it is the antithesis of the Christian spirit, of democracy, of freedom the American way.

Rightly understood it means that I must respect the other man's rights. It does not mean that I can do as I please. It does mean that I am not to interfere with another, to intimidate or discriminate. It does not mean that I am under no obligation to him. "My freedom stops where another's nose begins." I am not free to ignore his freedom, his welfare, and his best interests.

"Live and let live" implies the highest in personal, social and civic relationships. It suggests that I must order my life in such a way that it benefits others; that I have a moral obligation to my fellowman which cannot be abrogated. It means that I have no more right to desert my fellowman than a military post in battle. In either case, desertion is treasonable by Christian standards.

I am "my brother's keeper!"

"You shall love the Lord your God with all your heart, and with all your soul, and with all your mind. This is the first and great commandment. And a second is like it. You shall love your neighbor as yourself. On these two commandments depend all the law and the prophets" (Matthew 22:37-40).

§ *GOD REIGNS!*

*G*od has not abdicated!
The agony of our mid-twentieth century is evidence of the accuracy of the Bible's statements concerning the last days. And a mark of the nearness of the return of Jesus Christ!

The space race—the mad rush to stockpile atomic weapons—the frustration and futility of diplomacy—the unpredictable eruption of trouble spots like pus sacs—the increase of industrial tension—the acceleration of crime and festering social malignancy—the hot breath of nationalism and revolution—the sickening, unrelenting, inexorable threat of thermo-nuclear war—these are not the death rattle of Christian civilization. They are the birth pangs of Christian fulfillment! Universal trouble does not spell doom. It proclaims victory!

"The whole creation is on tiptoe to see the wonderful sight of the sons of God coming into their own. The world of creation cannot as yet see reality, yet it has been given hope. And the hope is that in the end the whole of created life will be rescued from the tyranny of change and decay, and have its share in that magnificent liberty which can only belong to the children of God. It is plain to anyone with eyes to see that at the present time all created life groans in a sort of universal travail...while we wait for that redemption of our bodies which will mean that at last we have realized our full sonship in Christ" (Romans 8:19-23 [Phillips version]).

Scoffers mock at the thought of Christ's return on the grounds that the Church has waited for this event for nineteen centuries. And this very scoffing fulfills Bible prediction. It is one of the signs (II Peter 3:3-5). Nothing is more certain than Christ's triumphant re-entry into history...and it is 1900 years nearer than when it was first promised! Today the whole universe languishes for the return of the Prince of Peace. "...and the kingdoms of this world shall become the kingdoms of our Lord and of His Christ."

Jesus Christ is Lord!

§ MAN CAN DEPEND UPON GOD

*T*he Christian says he believes God reigns, but he often acts as though God has abdicated! We profess to trust in God's overruling providence in the affairs of men and nations, but we live as though He had abandoned the world.

The Bible teaches by precept and example—thousands of precepts, thousands of examples—that God keeps in touch with His world and His people; that He is infinitely more interested than they in man's progress, individually and collectively. God is not only interested in the process of history. He is involved in it! And the outcome is completely in His control! It is human impertinence to talk as though God were impersonal, aloof, and disinterested. The Apostle declared quite emphatically that "God works in everything for good to them that love Him and are called according to His purpose" (Romans 8:28).

Why then do we ever give way to pessimism and despair? In our saner moments, we know beyond the peradventure of a doubt that God is always the Master of all circumstances, never the victim of any! He is never taken by surprise, never thwarted, never frustrated. *God is in charge!* Anxiety therefore is a kind of mistrust, a kind of challenge to God's integrity and fidelity. Anxiety means that we believe in the circumstances more than we believe in God! Things may look black at times, but God is always bigger than things.

Christian is not an ostrich. He doesn't bury his head in the sand. He faces the facts, black, ugly, discouraging though they be. Then He takes a long look at the supreme fact: the fact of Almighty God who is the Lord of the universe! Christian is realistic about circumstances. He is likewise realistic about God. Christian is a realist all the way, not just half the way.

"The God who made the world and everything in it, being Lord of heaven and earth...gives to all men life and breath and everything... made every nation of men to live on all the face of the earth, having determined their allotted periods and the boundaries of their habitation" (Acts 17:24-26).

§ THE RELEVANCE OF BLOOD

"*B*lood is the nation's number-one medicine in the saving of lives!" Startling words, thoughtful words, taken from *Lifeline*, the monthly bulletin of the Montgomery County, Maryland branch of American Red Cross.

Never were profounder words uttered. And they go to the very heart of the Hebrew-Christian tradition. That brief phrase spells out in scientific language the clue to the Christian dynamic—the core of the Christian message. Those words proclaim the Gospel in its purest form!

"The life is in the blood," declared Moses (Leviticus 17:11). The word "blood" occurs more than 440 times in the Bible: 340 times in the Old Testament and 102 in the New. The greatest day in Israel's calendar was "The Day of Atonement." The Passover was the most significant of her annual celebrations. Both have to do with the shedding of blood. Heart of Israel's worship was the blood sacrifice given by Moses to be administered by the Levitical Priesthood. The author of the epistle to the Hebrews declares, "Without shedding of blood there is no remission of sins."

"Covering" is the literal meaning of the word "atonement"— covering for sin. "Come now and let us reason together, saith the Lord; though your sins be as scarlet, they shall be as white as snow; though they be red like crimson, they shall be as wool" (Isaiah 1:18).

"I will keep the Passover," said Jesus to His disciples. And He was not referring to the mere celebration of an historic occasion. He meant to keep it literally, meant to fulfill it literally! Jesus Christ came to die! He was not surprised by the cross. It was not an unexpected, premature end to an otherwise phenomenal life. On the contrary, the cross was the purpose of His coming. He was born to be crucified!

His legacy was left us at the Last Supper. "This is My body broken for you...My blood shed for the remission of sins." This is the heart of Christian worship. It is God's answer to man's deepest need. God's remedy for man's sin! "The blood of Jesus Christ, God's Son, cleanseth from all sin."

§ *OUR DEEPEST NEED*

*W*hy didn't Jesus wipe out human misery 1900 years ago?

According to the record He gave sight to three blind men. Why not eliminate blindness? He touched cripples and they walked. He made the deaf to hear, the dumb to speak. Why not do this for all cripples, for all who were deaf or dumb? He fed thousands with a few scraps of food, and there were baskets full left over. Why should anyone have to go hungry? For that matter the record says He raised three people from the dead. Why not bring everyone back to life, cancel out death completely?

Had He reached the limits of His power? Did He handle as many cases as He was able and have to leave the rest to their misery?

He said, "No man takes My life from Me; I lay it down of Myself, I take it up again. I have the power to lay it down and take it up." If so, why did He allow Himself to be crucified? Why didn't He stay alive, eliminate sickness, disease, poverty, misery and death in His generation...and permanently!

Because He was the Great Physician! He knew men's misery is a symptom. He knew the disease itself was sin, and the only cure for the disease was the cross. His mission was the cross. His cure for the disease was the shedding of His blood. He was born to be crucified!

Thank God for medical science that refuses to be satisfied simply with treatment that helps man endure illness...that does not stop until it finds a cure. Jesus could have dealt only with symptoms, kept pumping life and health back into man generation by generation ad infinitum...but so what? He came to cure the disease of sin altogether, to eliminate the virus so man would no longer be infected by it forever! He did precisely this! That's the whole point of Easter's celebration!

Of course a cure doesn't work unless a man takes it! Obviously! What pathetic absurdity to see man still preoccupied with the symptoms, still trying to solve his sociological problems, while he ignores the affliction that produces them!

"Behold the Lamb of God which taketh away the sin of the world!" (John 1:29).

§ *GET AT THE RIGHT SIDE*

*T*here are three sides to every question! Not just two sides—*Three!* Your side, the other fellow's side—and the *right side*! Only real cure for any problem is to discover and apply the right side!

This is the crux of the matter! We're not really interested in the right side! We're interested in our side. The other fellow's interested in his side. Result: impasse; deadlock. Deadlocks are resolved only by concession and expediency. Real issue is lost in foolish finagling, plotting, scheming. And the whole system moves along on a lower, instead of a higher level. Like little boys on a vacant lot: "I won't let you use my ball unless you let me pitch." You don't get the best pitcher that way! And each side harbors a grudge, regrets concessions it has been forced to make, and burns with resentment deep down in. Like a volcano, resentments seethe and smolder some day to erupt in worse conflagration.

Here are a husband and wife not getting along. He has his side; she hers. Neither wants to give in...until finally they have to out of sheer necessity in order to live together. So concessions are made. Each one reluctantly gives in part way. Neither can quite forget. Each feels he is right. Then some silly little argument sets it off again, worse than before. Buried grudges explode to the surface, driving them wider and wider apart. Until divorce is all that's left... There is a third side to that! The right side! God's side! It is the only possible remedy. It would work if each would take that side. That would settle it once for all, lift the whole thing to a new level.

Here's conflict in industry. Management has its side. Labor, too! Each fights to maintain its "rights." *Deadlock!* Then they begin to whittle, jockey, conspire. Finally, agreement; but with each side giving in as little as possible and cutting in on the other as much as possible. Both cherish the day they can regain what they lost in concessions granted out of sheer expediency. Problems not solved. Actually increased! In the long run the conflict is not settled, just postponed. Resentments burn quietly, deeply, explosively. Expediency will never cure. It only stops the headache temporarily, lets the disease run its course. We need clean, sharp, final solutions.

We've got to learn to seek the right side to every question: home, business, industry, nation, world. There's no alternative...but chaos!

"Submit yourselves one to another in reverence for God" (Ephesians 5:21).

§ *POINT OF NO RETURN*

*I*t is not the big decision, the complicated, elaborate one, that determines a man's destiny. It's the little every day simple choices that set the stage, tune a man's will, pre-determine what his big decisions will be in the pinches! Generally speaking big decisions are few and far between. And how a man reacts, what he does with the big issues, is already decided on the basis of the many little choices he makes from day to day. Little choices determine habit. Habit carves and molds character. Character makes the big decisions!

This is illustrated by a simple little gadget which contributed immeasurably to the success of transoceanic flying. It is called the "How Goes It chart." In the operations compartment of the plane the pilot has a chart of the perfect voyage (assuming perfect flying conditions, a perfect machine and perfect handling). It is there for the captain to measure the success of his own flight. As he compares his flight with the perfect one he has any number of opportunities to choose to return to His point of departure if he feels his trip is not "adding up" to the perfect schedule. However, at a point on the chart there is a line drawn. This is called "The Point of No Return!" Once a pilot has passed that point he has *no alternative* but to go on, regardless of what happens!

It works that way in life too! Little choices a man makes day after day, none of which may seem strategic or significant in itself, added together reveal a tendency, a direction, a mind-set! Each succeeding choice carves the pattern more deeply. Each succeeding choice sets the direction more firmly. Until it crystallizes! That is the point of no return in that area. A man's will has been conditioned to choose a certain way. He becomes the product of his simple choices. The big ones are made on that basis!

This is preeminently true of a man's relationship to Christ. He hears the Word of God over and over—and does nothing! At no time does there seem to be any great issue involved. He gets used to hearing and *doing nothing*! It becomes easier and easier to hear without hearing; to see without seeing; to be moved and not decide! Until at last nothing bothers him. He does not hear, or see, nor can he be moved. Beware of the point of no return!

"Now is the acceptable time...now is the day of salvation!" (II Corinthians 6:2).

§ HARDBOILED FACTS

*O*ne reason Christianity ought to have a certain strong appeal for the hard-headed businessman in the twentieth century is that it deals with hardboiled facts! It's not a matter of vague, nebulous thinking by theologians far removed from the work-a-day world of profit and loss and competition. Christian faith did not originate with long-haired religionists! Nor did it begin with philosophical speculation. The Bible is not a record of man's highest and best thoughts about God. There's nothing hypothetical nor speculative about the historic Christian faith.

Christianity did not begin with ideas! It began with events! It was born out of a startling, staggering, globe-shaking events! The faith of the Christian man is not based upon the thinking of men. It is founded upon the deeds of God! "God so loved the world that He gave His only begotten Son...." God did something! That's the heart of Christianity! Not man trying to find God, trying to figure God out, but God loving man—and doing something about it!

God Himself, in the Person of Jesus Christ, actually, literally invaded human history...at a certain time, in a certain place, under certain circumstances. Those are the stubborn facts! Upon these, Christian faith stands. Having lived a perfect life, Jesus Christ was tried, condemned and crucified. He died on a cross! This is what He came to do! He said so Himself. Time after time He tried to get it over to His disciples that He was to die!

His enemies put Him in a tomb, rolled a stone over the entrance, sealed it with the Roman Imperial seal, stationed the Temple guard about it! They were taking no chances! They wanted to make sure that body stayed in the grave. Their elaborate precautions were wasted! No grave could hold Him! The morning of the third day, the first day of the week, the tomb was empty; the body was gone! His enemies would have paid any price to recover that body. It would have settled this thing once and for all! But there was no body to be had! After forty days He appeared again and again! To the women; to two disciples; to the Eleven; to more than five hundred at once...in a body of flesh and bone! They never expected to see Him again. They were amazed. Incredulous! But they could not deny their senses. He was there; He ate with them. Thomas saw the nail prints in His hands, the spear wound in His side!

Not the teaching of Jesus, *but the death and Resurrection!* That is the heart and soul of the Christian faith. That was the Apostolic message. That is the Gospel—the Good News!

"...Christ died for our sins according to the Scriptures; And that He was buried; and that He rose again the third day according to the Scriptures" (I Corinthians 15:3, 4).

§ *EASTER'S SECRET*

*E*vents, not ideas, comprise the foundation of Christian faith. Easter has to do with events, not with theories or doctrines or ethics. Easter commemorates two cosmic, globe-shaking events! Not the things Jesus said, but the things Jesus did are the solid rock upon which the belief of the Christian man rests. This is the strength of Christian faith!

Christianity begins with *facts*, not fancies and foibles. What Jesus said was important; but apart from what He did, what He said was meaningless. For the things Jesus said pointed men to their need in order that they might trust what He had come to do for them. He was a Teacher—the greatest! His life was exemplary—the finest and the purest! But the whole point to His teaching and His life was the work He had come to do for man! That work was to offer Himself as a Sacrifice for sin: the sin of the world; the sin of every man who ever lived. Jesus came into the world as "the Lamb of God that taketh away sin."

Everything He said was designed to show men their need of a Savior: His qualifications as a Savior; His purpose to be their Savior; and that without Him as Savior men were doomed! His penetrating teaching, His purity of life revealed man's spiritual bankruptcy and need. Like an X-ray the words of Jesus and the perfection of Jesus exposed the pride and greed and selfishness and envy and lust and covetousnes that infected the human heart...even the heart of the most religious men! They had made religion a means of avoiding God and evading the real issue of holiness. They had invented their own religion, leaving God outside!

To Jesus true religion was not a matter of rules and regulations. It was not a matter of external righteousness, of do's and don'ts. It was a matter of inward peace and purity. He knew that evil men could act decently, if acting decently made it possible for them to achieve their evil purposes. He knew religious men could wear a cloak of piety and have hearts filled with evil ambition and desire. Jesus came to provide a cure for the malignancy in the human heart. He came into the world as Redeemer, to do a redemptive work. The point of His coming was the cross! There is no hope in the teaching of Jesus, or the life of Jesus, without the death and Resurrection of Jesus!

This is the real significance of Good Friday and Easter. These days commemorate the two greatest events in human history: the death and Resurrection of Jesus Christ.

This is the hope of Easter: "Christ died for our sins; He was raised again for our justification."

§ THE CRUX OF HISTORY

The most phenomenal fact in history is the crucifixion of Jesus Christ. It is utterly inexplicable by natural standards. How do you explain the fact that humanity crucified the only perfect Man who ever lived? It was not a mistake! On the contrary it was a monstrous, premeditated scheme. It was thought out carefully, maliciously. It certainly was not an accident! Nor was He a martyr! Nothing is farther from the truth. A martyr is the victim of his enemies and his death. Jesus Christ was the Master of His. He was never victimized. He anticipated the cross. He knew it was His primary objective!

There were many amazing things about the death of Jesus Christ: three hours of darkness from noon to three, with the sun at its zenith; the earthquake splitting open graves; the veil in the temple rent from top to bottom. But most astounding was the death itself! Crucifixion was the most horrible means of capital punishment. It was a penalty reserved for the worst criminals, so terrible that no Roman citizen could be crucified no matter how atrocious his crime. What made it horrible was the suspense. It meant slow, maddening, painful, lingering death. The crucified man literally died of sheer exhaustion. The body dehydrated. Normally it took several days. Jesus died in a few short hours! The suddenness of it shocked the Roman soldiers. They were amazed by it! They cried out, "Surely this was the Son of God!" What killed Him? Why did He die? The cross hadn't done it.

Recall they had tried to take Him on several occasions previously and had failed. He escaped every time. But in the Garden of Gethsemane He said His time had come. He turned Himself over to them without a struggle. Previously He had said, "No man taketh My life from Me. I lay it down of Myself. I have the power to lay it down and the power to take it up again." Standing before Pilate, Jesus said, "You have no power over Me whatever except it were given you from above." No power on earth could have taken the life of Jesus Christ if He had not wanted it to. Proof of that lies in the fact that though they put His corpse in a tomb, three days later He came forth—resurrected!

When you understand the secret of His death, you have the key to life itself! He came to die. That was His supreme purpose. And He accomplished it! On the cross it is recorded He spoke seven times. Last of His words was the single exclamation: "Finished." The next statement as the record puts it is: "When He had said this He yielded up His spirit." That's why He died! By the sheer, deliberate act of His will He laid down His life to purchase redemption for man. He died that you and I might live. Without His death we have no hope.

Have you ever thanked Him for dying for you?

§ *THE SUPREME ACT OF FAITH*

*E*aster is not the expression of some fond but vain anticipation, some incredible, ethereal hope unfulfilled. It is the celebration of a cosmic historical fact: the actual, literal, bodily Resurrection of Jesus Christ!

Late Thursday night, first century A.D., they took Him prisoner while He was praying in Gethsemane. At the home of Annas and Caiaphas He was perfunctorily tried and condemned. Early Friday morning, just as it began to dawn, they took Him bound to the Praetorium where Pilate, Provincial Governor, ruled. Between Herod and Pilate there ensued a series of ridiculous, diabolical prostitutions of justice. It ended with Christ condemned to death by crucifixion. The penalty was instantly carried out. In a few hours His broken body hung limp and dead on the cross. They took it down; wrapped it in burial linen; put it in a tomb. They rolled a huge stone over the entrance, applied the official seal of Imperial Rome and stationed a platoon of guards. Early Sunday morning some of His disciples came to the tomb. To their shock and chagrin the tomb was empty. The stone was removed. The seal was broken. The body was gone. The wrappings were on the slab in the shape of the body.

Where was the body? The enemies of Christ would have paid any price to retrieve it. It would have established once and for all their claim that He was an impostor. Their only recourse was to pay the Roman soldiers to lie, to say that the body had been stolen by His disciples while they slept. If they were asleep, how did they know what happened? Stupid efforts of men to cover the truth!

It was not fiction! It was solid fact! Jesus had risen from the dead as He said He would. They didn't believe Him. Even His disciples disbelieved this! So it was no illusion when they saw Him. At first when He appeared they thought He was a ghost. He proved the contrary by letting them handle Him, feel His flesh and bone, put a finger in the nail holes in His hands. He ate their food. Ghosts don't eat fish and bread. This was real! For forty days He walked the earth and showed Himself alive by "many infallible proofs." He appeared to many, including more than five hundred on one occasion.

The Resurrection fact is thoroughly substantiated by evidence. No fact of history stands more completely verified. Jesus Christ is not a dead martyr. He's a living Savior! He's alive today! He's not just fact in history. He's a present, contemporary reality in the experience of Christians. He defeated man's worst enemy—*death*. He robbed victory from the grave. He has life to offer—eternal life. It's a gift for all who will have it! You can't earn it, but you may have it free! Have you received the gift of eternal life? Will you? Now?

§ FAITH THAT TRIUMPHS

*T*he point of Easter is that *righteousness triumphs!* Evil may have its ugly little day, but goodness wins! Satanic forces may win a battle or two, but Godly forces win the war. That's Easter!

It looked for a while as if sin were the victor: Christ on the cross; righteousness and love and truth crucified; purity impaled on a tree. Downcast—dejected—desperate must have been the disciples as they looked at the battered, broken, bleeding body of their beloved Master hanging limp and beaten and hopeless. Darkness, thick, blackness you could feel, clammy darkness, blotted out the sun for three hours when it was at its zenith from noon to three. It certainly looked like the end of justice and mercy and truth and purity. It must have seemed useless to do right, if even Jesus Christ Himself could not win.

But the sun broke upon an empty tomb three days later...and blazoned the fact that righteousness had triumphed! Certainly a man gets weary in well-doing. It so often looks like all the odds are on the other side: all the battles go against him; evil men prosper; injustice and inequity reign; sin parades and bloats and brags. Purity is mocked. Even in the "best" circles a man may be ridiculed if he takes righteousness too seriously. (Teenagers are not the only ones that call a man "square" when he does not conform.) Filthy jokes, lewd innuendoes, profanity fill the air at some sales meetings, board meetings, service clubs, and men's luncheons. Temperance is scorned as an umbrella carrying, blue-nosed queer in a long black coat and high hat. Nothing new about this. It was true about 1900 years ago. It put Christ, the sinless Son of God, on the cross. Wickedness could not stomach His perfection, so wickedness crucified Him.

We might as well face it, man: In our day, in this freedom-loving land of ours, amid the luxury and opulence that abounds, it's an uphill battle to stand for righteousness. A man can take an awful beating from a crowd when he does, but this is the kind of greatness our world needs today: men who have a flash point against sin. Men who dare to stand against the tide. Men who won't go along with the crowd at the terrible expense of purity. It will cost something! But this is our only hope! And it will win!

"Righteousness exalteth a nation, but sin is a reproach to any people" (Proverbs 14:34); "Therefore;...be ye stedfast, unmoveable, always abounding in the work of the Lord, forasmuch as you know that your labor is not in vain in the Lord" (I Corinthians 15:58).

§ ALWAYS TOO SOON TO DESPAIR

*I*f Judas had only waited! It would have meant only three days. Bitter days perhaps, with Jesus in the tomb, but unbelievably short days in the light of the Resurrection. But he didn't wait! He cast the thirty pieces of silver to the ground, went out and hanged himself because he thought Christ was dead forever. Judas committed the final, fatal error. He despaired of God—and of himself. And he didn't see the Resurrection!

That is the worst sin: to despair of God. Second worst is to despair of one's self. Because self-despair implies despair of God: "My problem is too big for God, or too small. My sin is too black. My deed incurable." Too big for God? Too black, incurable? For God? Sometimes we act like God is dead. We get so discouraged with ourselves. We can't understand the things we do that we shouldn't; the things we neglect we ought to do. It's so easy to fail sometimes. "Nobody can be as bad as I. Nobody else would make such a mistake. No one else could fail like I've failed." Too often we reason that way, and that leads to despair of God and self. It's dead wrong!

Hopelessness is not a Christian word. It doesn't belong in a Christian's vocabulary. No situation, sin, failure, is hopeless, unless you despair of self and God. A man is never a failure, no matter how often he fails; until he admits it. Until he gives in—or gives up.

Someone once asked James J. Corbett during his colorful career, "What is most important for a man to do to become champion?" Corbett replied, "Fight one more round!" "When Walt Disney applied at the *Kansas City Star* for a job as artist, the editor sent him away urging him to give up his idea. Robert L. Ripley was fired from the first three newspapers on which he worked. Zane Grey didn't sell a story his first five years of writing. First time George Gershwin played the piano in public, they laughed him off the stage. The U.S. Navy retired Richard Byrd at 28 because of a broken ankle. He decided to become an aviator and crashed twice while learning, once hit another plane head-on. But he went another round" (*Friendly Chat*, Baker Oil Tools).

"Beaten paths are for beaten men" (*Autonews*, editorial). Rivers grow crooked by dodging difficulties. So do men. Roads wind when they take the line of least resistance, and they carry little traffic. Broad highways blast through every barrier and carry the world's business. It is never too late to let God into a situation. It is always too soon to despair. God is not dead. With God, all things are possible. He is the God of the impossible! Keep looking up!

§ INVINCIBLE!

*A*s a sequel to Easter, consider one of the most stupendous statements in the New Testament, one of those overwhelming promises of God to man! "Now unto Him who is able to do exceedingly abundantly above all that we ask or think..." (Ephesians 3:20). This is the follow-through of the Resurrection.

"Now unto Him who is able...!" Emphasis on God's ability! Nothing is too hard for Him. He is the God of the impossible! He is able to perform that which He has promised. Absolutely no limit to the resources of God! "Now unto Him who is able to do...." Not a God who can but won't, but a God of action. Not a remote, detached, indifferent deity, but a God who takes a personal interest in His world and will do something about it! This is preeminent in the Bible. He is a working God. He has made Himself known by deeds—not merely through idea and concept familiar only to the theologian. He is the God of the common man.

"...able to do all that we ask or think..." which apart from anything else that can be said is in itself tremendous. But the promise does not stop there. "...able to do more than we ask or think." Nor is that the limit of the promise: "...abundantly more than we ask or think." And that is not the end of this fabulous proposition. "Now unto Him who is able to do exceedingly abundantly above all we ask or think." God's doings are way out ahead of man! His ways are not our ways, nor His thoughts ours. For "as high as the heaven is above the earth" so are His ways—His thoughts—above ours!

A wonderful promise, but utterly meaningless if you stop quoting at that point. Only as you consider the last part of the promise does it make sense: "Now unto Him who is able to do exceedingly abundantly above all that we ask or think according to the power that worketh in us!" That is the key! God does not work in a vacuum. God does not work in the abstract. God works through men! God's method is men, not machinery. His unlimited power and resources are available... but useful only as there are men committed to let God do His work through them. This is the down-to-earth, practical side of Christianity. God does His work in the world through men. When God has a job to do He looks for a man! When God finds a man as a channel, there is no limit to what He can do through that man! The resources are God's; the means is the man: God's man—committed!

Speaking at a men's conference in Sacramento, former Governor Langlie of Washington said, "The worst fear in the church is fear of commitment. Men are afraid to commit themselves to Christ, afraid of what it will cost!" But this is the answer to an explosive and unsettled world: Men who are unconditionally committed to Christ. As unconditionally committed to Him as hard-core Communists are to their cause.

"I beseech you therefore, brethren, by the mercies of God to present your bodies a living sacrifice, wholly acceptable to God... your reasonable service" (Romans 12:1).

§ IRRATIONAL REJECTION

*W*hy do men reject Jesus Christ? What is there about Him that causes some men to get so angry, so adamant, so abusive when His Name is mentioned? What is there that makes men, intelligent, cultured, good men take His Name in vain? Why is this Name bandied about loosely in the finest clubs and offices? Why does the Name of Jesus Christ so often, so consistently often, so unconsciously often, pass through the lips of men as a curse, a by-word? And to make matters worse nobody ever seems to care! Let this beautiful Name be associated with obscene jokes, filthy conversation, low life... It never bothers anybody!

What quiet—cultured—intelligent—subtle—Godless blasphemy!

What did Jesus Christ ever do that men should hate Him? There is nothing in the record against Him. Even His bitterest enemies were forced to employ false witnesses to build a case against Him! Nobody who touched His life saw a trace of weakness in Him. There's no record of any sin which He committed. There's no evidence of any mistake, any failure, any slightest deviations from perfection in His life! He did nothing but good deeds for men. He was utterly selfless, completely at the disposal of others. He never once asked for anything for Himself, defended Himself, protected Himself! His life was spent for others. He was really expendable! Wherever there was a need, there Christ was available, pouring out His life to supply it. He never accumulated a thing, never demanded anything, never owned anything! Yet real Communists hate Him, despise Him, and try to disinherit Him in the minds of those who love and follow Him. Communists have slaughtered men indiscriminately for being followers of Jesus Christ. His life was the epitome, the quintessence of virtue. His teaching laid the foundation of everything that is important and basic and good in the American way of life...but Americans by the millions ignore Him!

Why is it that many businessmen don't want Jesus Christ? Why will they say, "I believe in God—but none of this belief in Jesus stuff!" What is the explanation for this almost vicious rebellion against Him? Or else—if not vicious rebellion, the indolence, indifference, neglect of Him...which is worse, if anything, than outright rebellion! What of your own heart? What place do you give to Jesus Christ? Do you hate Him? Or do you quietly ignore Him? Or do you just use His Name as a curse to express anger, bitterness, hate, or simply to be forceful in your conversation?

"He that is not for Me is against Me!" (Jesus Christ).

§ DEATH IS FOR REAL

"*Drive slowly. Death is so permanent!*" This sign startled me the other day while I was driving from a pastoral call. Death is so permanent!

Recently it was my duty to conduct the funeral service for a local businessman. Many of his friends were present, most of them business and professional men like himself, to pay their last respects. The funeral was over in twenty minutes. Slowly the crowd moved past the casket out into the bright sunshine of a beautiful afternoon. I watched from my place at the casket's head. When I came from the chapel later, the contrast was staggering. In the chapel, those men sat with serious faces, thoughtful, considerate. They must have wondered about death. It had come so suddenly to this friend...

He had gone to work as usual a few mornings before, apparently as well as ever. Forty-five minutes after he left home he was dead at his desk. Surely these friends were thinking of that as we went through the service! But it was soon dismissed as they moved out of the chapel, dismissed like an unwanted cloud over the sun. Gaily they conversed in little groups on the lawn of the cemetery. And from all appearances, you would think that none of them entertained a thought that this could happen to them. Like a false alarm they pushed it out of their minds.

Here's a real dilemma! It's good business to prepare for an emergency. Good business management maintains reserve funds to cover emergencies. You cannot avoid an emergency by ignoring it. You meet it by facing it, anticipating it. Yet intelligent men, with sharp business minds, go through life indifferent to the greatest emergency of all. They prepare for dozens of other emergencies which may never occur, but they neglect to prepare their souls for the one inevitable appointment each must keep. Death is so permanent!

This is pitiful in the light of the gracious provision God has made available for everyone in the Bible. Nothing is clearer; nothing is simpler; than the promise of eternal life to all who will receive it. Ponder it a moment...

"What shall it profit a man if he gain the whole world and lose his own soul?" (Matthew 16:26).

§ *COOPERATION*

*E*fficient enterprise demands a *top man*! One who has the last word, the final say. One in whom resides executive authority, who has power to decide, to act. One to carry responsibility. It also demands a clearly defined purpose: to build cars, publish periodicals, sell furniture, money and banking, advertising, etc.

Assuming a good man at the top—and a worthwhile purpose—one other thing is absolutely imperative: the whole-hearted cooperation and support of all subordinates. Only as the men and women "underneath" in business and industry willingly cooperate with the "top brass" and the purpose, can an enterprise thrive, grow, prosper. No business can succeed when subordinates are rebellious or out of harmony with its administration and purpose. Even one employee not in accord is like sand in machinery where oil should be. Anarchy does not work in business any more than in government, home, school, or club. Anarchy is the archenemy of all progress!

See God's viewpoint for a minute: Here's a world designed by Him, with clear, high purpose to benefit His supreme creature—man! But things aren't clicking! There's a fly in the ointment... In all this cosmic

Divine enterprise there's one note of disharmony. Insubordination on the part of the one whom God loves most—man. Human nature is the only part of creation that ignores the Head and purpose. The planets revolve in their courses according to His plan. Plant life, animal life, sun, moon, earth, all function in strictest conformity to the will and purpose of the Creator. Only man "goes his own way...."

Nothing wrong with atomic fission. It's the basic structure of life. For thousands of years man has benefited from it—until he discovered it. Now it's his deadly foe. Fact is, man seems adept at using good things in bad ways: Money, food, drink, love, sex, etc. ad infinitum. Everybody thinking in terms of what he can get out of life, not what he can put in. Everybody, or most everybody, ignoring God, busy with his own plans, schemes, schedules.

Frankly, in this pattern God is just an imposition! What would you do if you were God? How would you run your business in this way? The place to start, of course, is for each of us, beginning with me, with you, to live with God and His will.

"Seek ye first the Kingdom of God, and His righteousness..." (Matthew 6:33).

§ *EFFICIENCY*

*E*ffective living, in simplest terms, is just a matter of right relationships. At bottom it simply means getting along together. Good home life depends on right relationships between man and wife, brother and sister, parent and child. Business and industry likewise demand this basic principle: right relations between employees; between employees and management; and within management itself.

Carry it out to every area of life: club, nation, world; and it boils down to this: good relationships promote efficiency, happiness, productivity. Frictionless living is the secret. The wider the sphere of good relationships, the better the business. That's why "Good Will" can be put on the balance sheet as an asset. That's the justification of "Public Relations." Because all these areas of life are tied together: good home life reflects in office and shop. Disharmony at home is transmitted to the job...and vice versa.

The important thing to remember is that there are primary and secondary relationships. Some are more important than others. Some demand first consideration over others. In the home for example, it is more important that the children be right with the parents than with each other. Assuming good parents, it would be wrong for children to line up together against them. In fact, the surest way for children to be right with each other, to enjoy life at its best in the home is to be right with the parents.

In business the relationship between labor and management is primary. It is more important that employees be right with management than that they be right with each other. Surest way for employees to be right with each other, to enjoy the best in their work, to get the most out of it, is to be right with the management—assuming, of course, good management. Surest way to disrupt efficiency, to curtail production, to destroy harmony in home or business, is for children to stand together against parents—for employees to stand against management. That's anarchy! Keep these relationships in line: primary and secondary. The whole fabric of life is enriched, energized, harmonized, strengthened.

There is one relationship above all others, absolutely primary, the foundation for all others: a man's relationship to his God. Surest formula for peace all down the line—world, nation, business, home— is for every man to be right with the Lord. That's the key.

"Seek ye first the Kingdom of God and His righteousness and all these things will be added unto you" (Matthew 6:33).

§ *POWER THAT CHANGES MAN*

*P*ut down all the troubles of the world! Corruption—crime— immorality—divorce—economic inequality—social injustice— war—etc.—etc. Draw a line; add them up... The sum total of all the agony, misery, and tragedy in the world is *sin*. Trace all these things back to their source. You'll find they originate in the human heart.

Get even closer home than that! What of your own life? Add up all your real problems. You'll discover the real problem is yourself. Sin in the heart is at the bottom of all your troubles—and mine! That is what really sets us back, whips us. That is why Jesus Christ is the only adequate solution to the world problem...to our personal need. Because He is the only One who has an answer to sin! He declared, and experience confirms it, that the source of all man's grief is the heart. That it is not so much a man's conduct as it is his nature that is wrong. Not what a man does, but what He is—inside. Man is not a sinner because he sins; he sins because he is a sinner! The bitter root of sin in his heart infects his whole life.

A man may be able to regulate and order his conduct, make it come out pretty ethically, but what he can't do is change his nature. He can change what he does, up to a point, but he can't change what he is. This is the crux of the problem. Something inside him keeps him from being, doing, saying his best. It's a constant struggle, plagued with failure!

Jesus Christ begins here with a man—with his nature, what he is. Jesus Christ changes a man from within. Puts within him a new nature that has no affinity with sin. Actually it is the nature of Christ Himself. He does not ask a man to reform. He transforms the man by the power of God...regenerates him. Gives him a new birth. This is, and has been down through the centuries, the unique and distinct claim of the Church of Jesus Christ. This is the historic and unadulterated message: the Gospel. No man struggling to reform himself, but God transforming man by Divine grace.

"Christ died for our sins!" That is the tremendous, colossal, stupendous, staggering claim of the Bible. There is in His death power, sufficient power, to cleanse sin from a man's heart, to bring forgiveness with God. There is transforming power in the cross of Christ. Any man who wants it, who asks for it, who consents to it, can—and will—experience this power of forgiveness and cleansing in his life. He will experience the invasion of his life by the eternal life of God Himself. Incredible, but true! This is Christianity! Literally, actually, honestly, this power of God—purging, cleansing, sanctifying power—is available to you. At the moment you really want it, ask for it; you will receive it. God has promised. His promises are inviolate, immutable!

If you have never really heeded the Gospel, why not at this moment! Before you put this book down. Why not run a real test on the claims of Jesus Christ? Give Him a chance to prove what He wants to do for you. Let Him into your heart.

"But as many as received Him, to them gave He power to become the sons of God..." (John 1:12); "If any man be in Christ he is a new creature ..." (II Corinthians 5:17).

§ *QUITTER?*

"*It is always too soon to quit!*" This sound advice was given by W. J. Cameron on the *Ford Sunday Evening Hour* some years ago. Henry Ford's formula for success was simple: "When you start a thing, finish it!" There are many excuses for quitting, none justifiable! A man may quit because he feels the thing he's doing is not worth finishing. What he's doing may not be important, but *he is*. It's what quitting will do to him that matters. Perhaps he loses his inspiration. He began in waves of excitement; then suddenly the inspiration's gone. The thing doesn't seem worth the effort. Temptation is to quit.

Maybe it won't make any difference to anyone else if he quits. But it will make a great deal of difference to himself. He's learning to be a quitter. It will be easier to quit next time. When a thing goes stale, after the inspiration is gone, that is the time to dig in and finish the job, simply for the sake of finishing, for the sake of self-respect. One of the clearest tests of a man's worthwhileness is his response to the uninspired moments—how he reacts to duty—what he does with drudgery. The fellow that depends on inspired moments rarely completes anything. He leaves a trail of unfinished, half-baked jobs behind. They stand as mute evidence of failure. What a pity to be dogged by unfinished business!

Men who count are those who refuse to quit, men who never hear the bell, men who never throw in the towel. They're always needed, always in demand. Nobody wants and nobody needs a quitter. Often a golf tournament is won on the last hole, the last putt. Football games have been won in the last thirty seconds by a team that was losing but refused to quit fighting. Business, industry move with the men who know how to see a thing through after the quitters have dropped out.

Look at Jesus Christ as He faced the cross. He had come to die— that was His earthly purpose. He "set His face like a flint" as He marched to His cross. "He finished the work God gave Him to do." Just before He died He cried out, "It is finished!" Without that finish there would be no hope for the world. In that finish there is hope for every failure, every sin, every need of man. In that finish is God's complete forgiveness: eternal life for every man who will receive it. Something hanging over your head now? Something started with big ideas, great plans and now it's faded? Inspiration drained off? Tempted to quit? Got a new idea? New inspiration? You'll lose that too—if you quit now.

"Men ought always to pray and never give up" (Luke 18:1 [Williams]).

§ ALCOHOLISM IS MORE THAN ILLNESS

"*T*he alcoholic makes the same use of the bottle as does the infant.... He organizes his life around it!" declared Harry Levinson, *The Executive's Anxious Age*, in IBM's THINK magazine.

That is a very accurate picture of an adult who remains a baby. Physically grown up, emotionally he's an infant or adolescent. He is as dependent on a bottle as the newborn in a maternity ward. And he requires as much nursing. He doesn't need sympathy...he needs a spanking! He needs the whine knocked out of him!

Let's quit supplying the alcoholic with ammunition for self-defense. He is already a genius at self-deception, self-justification. To be sure alcoholism is a sickness, *but* it is more than that! There is no other disease like it. It is caught only by those who drink! The alcoholic blames everybody but himself for his condition: his wife, the boss, his mother-in-law, circumstances, ad nauseam. Then he drinks to protect himself from these "enemies" who are trying to destroy him. Meanwhile some well-meaning sentimental do-gooder feeds his ego by comforting him as a sick person, overlooking the sin of conceit, self-pity and escapism.

Sure the alcoholic is sick, and weak, but thousands have been "cured" when they quit blaming others, and recognized they were responsible for the mess they were in; accepted this fact; admitted their inadequacy; and sought the help of One who was greater than they. The alcoholic, like the rest of us, is his own greatest enemy. When he sees this, admits it, turns to God for help (God uses others like members of Alcoholics Anonymous in this), he gets his answer—and it works.

"Be not deceived...neither thieves, nor covetous, nor drunkards, nor revilers, nor extortioners, shall inherit the kingdom of God" (I Corinthians 6:9, 10); "If any man be in Christ he is a new creature, old things are passed away" (II Corinthians 5:17).

§ *WHY WORRY?*

*T*houghts, not things, cause worry! Not the things in life, but how you look at them, makes the difference. Take an honest look at most of your concerns. Discover how unreal they are. Two things cause worry: (1) Thoughts about the past: the failure, defeat, mistakes, things left undone, things that ought not to have been done. (2) Thoughts about the future: what might happen tomorrow, next week. Neither of these can we touch. Because they do not really exist in fact, they exist only as you keep them in your mind. They are the seeds of worry, dread, fear, and confusion. Worry over such things which do not actually exist.

The wise man learns to take life as it comes, not as he thinks it may come. The foolish man worries only to discover when the time comes that it was unnecessary. Why borrow trouble unnecessarily, foolishly? The only real thing about life is the minute you're living right now. It's yours. Then the next and the next! The past is not yours and even the future is not yours. You get life a minute at a time. Take it that way! This does not mean that you do not plan wisely for the future. It does mean that you guarantee the future best by using the present intelligently. Clutter up the present by loading yourself down with worries of the past and future, thoughts about things over which you have no control. It cuts down your efficiency, drags on your energy, keeps you from being your best now. Worries about what you cannot control—the past and future—defeat the one thing you have control over—the present. That's the tragedy of borrowed trouble. Don't need it! Can't use it! But you pay heavy interest on it!

Here too the Gospel of Jesus Christ has the key to realism—to life. For it is only in the Gospel that men have hope for failure of the past and for the unknown of the future. The Gospel is the "power of God unto salvation." It has power to salvage a man, to turn past failures and defeats into lessons, to utilize the lessons for the present and future. "The blood of Jesus Christ, God's Son, cleanseth us from all sin." What could be better than that? Complete cleansing as though you had never sinned. That's the unbelievable promise of the Gospel: thorough provision for everything in the past, blotted out, forgotten in the grace of God.

God is able to take the wrecks, the failures, the defeats, the sin of past days and actually turn them for good today. Only the Gospel can do it! Have you ever experienced the power of God in the Gospel? The power that can make you over? Turn your defeats into victories today? Make you really effective in your work now? Why not give this Gospel a try?

"All things work together for good to them that love God, to them that are the called according to His purpose" (Romans 8:28).

§ *ON GROWING OLD*

*Y*ou're going to meet an old man someday! Down the road ahead—ten, twenty, thirty years—waiting there for you. You'll be catching up with him. What kind of an old man will he be? He may be a seasoned, soft, gracious fellow, a gentleman that has grown old gracefully; surrounded by hosts of friends, friends who call him blessed because of what his life has meant to them. He may be a bitter, disillusioned, dried-up, cynical old buzzard without a good word for anybody, soured, friendless and alone.

The kind of an old man you will meet depends entirely on yourself. Because that old man will be you. He'll be the composite of everything you do, say and think today; tomorrow. His mind will be set in a mold you have made by your attitudes. His heart will be turning out what you've been putting in. Every little thought, every deed goes into this old man. He'll be exactly what you make him. Nothing more, nothing less. It's up to you. You'll have no one else to credit or blame.

Every day in every way you are becoming more and more like yourself. Amazing, but true! You're getting to look more like yourself; think more like yourself; talk more like yourself. You're becoming yourself more and more. Live only in terms of what you're getting out of life. The old man gets smaller, drier, harder, crabbier, more self-centered. Open your life to others: think in terms of what you can give, your contribution to life. The old man grows larger, softer, kindlier, greater.

Point to remember is that these things don't always tell immediately. But they'll show up sooner than you think. These little things, so unimportant now—attitudes, goals, ambitions, desires—are adding up inside where you can't see them, crystallizing in your heart and mind. Some day they'll harden into that old man. Nothing will be able to soften or change them. Time to take care of that old man is right now, today, this week. Examine his motives, attitudes, goals. Check up on him. Work him over while he's still plastic, still in a formative condition. Day comes awfully soon when it's too late. The hardness sets in worse than paralysis. Character crystallizes, sets, gels. That's the finish.

Any wise businessman takes inventory regularly. His merchandise isn't half so important as he is. Better take a bit of personal inventory too. We all need it in the light of Christ and His Word. You'll be much more likely to meet a splendid old fellow at the proper time, the fellow you'd like to be.

"Be not deceived; God is not mocked: for whatsoever a man soweth, that shall he also reap" (Galatians 6:7); "The path of the just is as the shining light, that shineth more and more unto the perfect day" (Proverbs 4:18).

§ *MORALITY IS NOT ENOUGH!*

$\mathcal{M}$orality is not enough! Something far more basic is needed! A moral man can be a secular man, and secularism is beating our world to death. Secularism is Godlessness! Witness a *Life* magazine editorial: "The worse enemy western civilization faces is within that civilization itself. Our $64 euphemism for it is 'secularism'...a blunter word is God-lessness." *Life* Editorial, April, 1949. The sad, sobering, staggering fact is that many of our best people, our moral people, are utterly secular... Godless. It is not a skid-row menace. It is a country club—Park Avenue menace.

Morality has to do with conduct—what a man does with externals. It's quite possible for a man to act all right outwardly: to order his con-duct ethically to achieve selfish ends. His conduct is good, but his heart is bad! Morality has to do with the horizontal relationships, a man's re-lationship with his fellowman. It can leave God out altogether! That's the subtle, ominous, deceptive danger in morality alone.

Spiritual men! That's the desperate need! Not pious frauds. Not men who are so heavenly minded they're no earthly good. God forbid! But real men, God-like, deep, spiritual men. Spirituality has to do with a man's motivation. Not so much what he does as why he does it! Spirituality is the root, the life-blood of morality. Without it morality can turn into a selfish "dog-eat-dog" tactic.

You can never trust a man whose motives are wrong no matter how fine his conduct may be. In fact the finer a man's conduct whose moti-vation is wrong, the more dangerous the man. Crooks operate that de-ception often, act nice to achieve evil ends. They order their conduct to deceive. The nicer the crook, the more dangerous! Morality affords a clever cover-up! Much social life and business life is operated at that low level too. People nice to you not for what they can do for you but with an eye to what they can get out of you.

You can always trust a man whose motives are right even though he may make mistakes. He's dependable and trustworthy when he's got honest motives. Spirituality has to do with the vertical relationship in life...a man's relationship to God. That's basic! Leave it out. Life decays, disintegrates from the inside out. Morality becomes a thin crust that cracks under pressure.

"Man looks on the outward appearance...but God looks on the heart" (I Samuel 16:7); "Out of the heart are the issues of life" (Proverbs 4:23).

§ GETTING OR GIVING?

*W*here's the accent in your life? On giving?...or getting? Having trouble with yourself? Ulcers? Nine chances out of ten there's too much *get* and too little *give* in you! It's the pressure of getting that ties a man up in knots! It's the pleasure of giving that eases him out into personal freedom and efficiency.

Take this candid shot of a very familiar experience: The scene is a Service Club in a large city. The occasion is a report by the committee on Thanksgiving baskets to poor families. Bubbling over with sheer pleasure the chairman, a local C.P.A., tells of the thrill the committee received as they delivered the baskets the week before. He tries to describe the unbelief in the eyes of a care-worn mother as she was handed the basket filled with turkey and all the trimmings. He tells about the uninhibited excitement of the kiddies as they crowded around, eyes bulging, trying to get a peek into the baskets. He pictures the speechless gratitude of a family that had expected to have beans for Thanksgiving. With undisguised emotion the chairman says something like this: "This was the greatest! I'll never forget this experience. It does something for a man to see how much a little food means to those people. We got a 'bigger bang' out of giving those baskets than they did receiving them! Let's put out twice as many baskets for Christmas!"

As he speaks—the whole club gets a lift from this heartwarming report. Every man feels the downright thrill of *giving*! Of course! Jesus Christ makes sense when He declares, "It is more blessed to give than it is to receive."

Man was meant to be a channel, not a reservoir! The man that bottles up his blessings discovers that they turn rancid and bitter. When a man shuts up the out-go in his life he stagnates. His life gets clogged! When he lets go, opens the channel, he mellows and matures. Pity the sour, dried-up, grumpy, touchy, fussy men who put the accent on *getting* in life!

"Give, and it shall be given unto you; good measure, pressed down, and shaken together, and running over..." (Luke 6:38).

§ *STEWARD OR SQUATTER?*

*H*ow a man looks at life makes all the difference in the world in that man's efficiency and production! A sense of stewardship about life is a man's more dynamic incentive. Rightly understood it stimulates the very best in a man; provokes top-level action and creative thinking. Stewardship takes life as a trust from God! A man comes into the world with nothing. All the raw materials are here for him to use. He can make the most of them; or he can piddle away opportunity and go through life amounting to zero with the edges rubbed off. The higher a man's goals, the greater the incentive that prods him along, the wiser use he is going to make of the raw materials and the more productive he is bound to be!

Some men take these opportunities for granted: Such a man figures life owes him a living. He complains about every difficulty and criticizes every man who buys up his opportunities. He labels every success a "break." To this man who lives like a "squatter" instead of a steward, the fellow that gets ahead and makes something of life is just "lucky." He goes through life excusing himself, feeling sorry for himself, whining and whimpering like a spoiled child. And all the time he is missing every opportunity life offers him, begrudging the progress of others, and getting nowhere himself!

Meanwhile the man who takes his stewardship of life seriously handles his talent, time, strength and money as a trust from God. Stimulated by this sense of accountability he tries to put them to the best use, to invest them most wisely. This does not mean he invests only a certain amount God's way, then does as he pleases with the rest. It is a caricature of stewardship to give God (let us say 10%) and then use the balance without regard for one's accountability to God.

The Christian steward recognizes the Divine right of eminent domain! Stewardship involves all of life! God has a 100% claim on a man. Therefore he tries to use 100% God's way! He prayerfully considers what portion of his talent and time and money he should invest in the work of Christ in the world. But he is also prayerfully aware of his accountability to God in the use of the balance.

God delights in this kind of man! God uses such a man way out beyond the limits of his own ability and blesses him out of all proportion to his dedication. The blessing is one of actually feeling a partnership with God, entering into the Divine program in the world. All other investments are temporal...this one is eternal.

"Lay up for yourselves treasures in heaven..." (Matthew 6:20).

§ GETTING THE MOST OUT OF LIFE

*T*he thing a man strives for ultimately is self-fulfillment!

There are many ways of putting it but in the final analysis what a man wants most in life is to fulfill himself: to feel he has achieved something, exploited all the possibilities within him. He wants to get all there is out of life and put everything he can into it! If he's an eight cylinder man he wants to run on all eight! The real man cherishes the aim to be productive, to make an impact, to leave the world a better place because he's been in it. He wants to feel he has left a worthwhile deposit for posterity. He desires to find his niche, his place in the sun. He desires to be worth his weight in salt at least.

The question is, how can this be managed?

Is there a way a man can be sure he'll find his place? Or does this involve extreme risk with the probability that a man will go through life fundamentally dissatisfied? Are most men destined to be square pegs in round holes all their lives? Are they doomed to end up "might-have-beens"? The answer is unequivocally no! It is unnecessary for a man to go through life unfulfilled. No man is doomed unless he chooses to be! And the secret lies not in aptitude tests, excellent as they may be. The secret is in a man's relation to God!

Man was made for fellowship with God, made to work God's way. Until he does he's a fish out of water! He's never himself until God rules in his heart. This is basic. God's order is as important in the heart of a man as it is in the heavens or in the physical world. God has a plan for every man's life. That plan includes all the details, and it promises complete fulfillment of the man. It makes the most of a man, draws the best out of him, utilizes his full potential. That man truly finds himself who gives himself to God to be God-possessed, God-directed, God-used!

So often we get the cart before the horse. A man tries to use God. Christianity becomes a way of getting what he wants and ends up in frustration and disillusionment. This is ridiculous on the surface, that a man should use God to realize his own ends, make God his servant. Of course such procedure does not pay off!

The paradox of life is that a man finds himself when he loses himself; becomes himself when he gives himself away to God; frees himself when he commits himself to God in unconditional obedience.

"Whosoever will save his life shall lose it, and whosoever shall lose his life for My sake shall find it" (Matthew 16:25).

§ *WHO'S ON TRIAL?*

*W*hat is your verdict of Jesus Christ? If you had been there at the turn of the centuries, what part would you have had in His liquidation?

Three classes of men were involved in His betrayal, trial and crucifixion: His enemies who were aggressive in their opposition; the great majority who were neutral; and His friends who were silent! The enemies took the initiative. Though few in number they made a lot of noise! Jesus' friends were not vocal; they were smitten dumb with fear which meant the neutral majority heard one voice, the vicious indictment of Christ's enemies. It was relatively simple to turn the apathetic crowd into a mob ruled by violence and hysteria! Neutrality is always dangerous!

Actually Jesus was tried six times: three by the religious leaders, twice by Pilate and once by Herod. Two occurred between midnight and dawn. Four came swiftly following sunrise. Jesus was rushed through these travesties which mark the most ignominious hours of human history: the one perfect sinless Man who ever lived; the One who had never committed a single selfish act, who gave Himself literally to men in a life dedicated to alleviate man's misery and cure man's sin; the Perfect One betrayed, condemned, crucified! Not one voice was raised that would justify this! The few witnesses who consented to speak bore false testimony. Not one shred of evidence! Not one iota of damning testimony. Yet they crucified Him!

This is a portrait of the world: Righteousness on a cross! Goodness liquidated! Christ crucified! "The world hates Me," said Jesus, "because I testify of it that its works are evil" (John 7:7). Nineteen hundred years separate us from that despicable, malicious hour. To this day there has never been a voice raised to indict Jesus Christ—not one shred of evidence against Him in nineteen hundred years—only false witnesses whose theories won't hold water. Yet today intelligent men, good men, religious men, reject Jesus Christ! Few are openly aggressive. The great majority are so easily influenced by a few vocal critics, and they crucify Christ by their indifference! And so often Jesus' friends remain silent, speechless when they might say a word for their Lord, a word that would turn neutral apathy into discipleship.

Question is where does each of us fit into the picture? Aggressive? Neutral? Speechless? Or a witness to Christ's glory? Actually Christ was not on trial! It was the chief priests, the scribes, the elders, Pilate and Herod, the masses! Their judgment against Christ was a verdict against themselves. Your heart is a courtroom. What is your verdict for Christ? Your eternal welfare depends on it!

"He that believeth on Him is not condemned..." (John 3:18).

§ IRREVOCABLE PROMISES

*H*ave you learned yet to count on the promises of God? Have you learned to trust them, reckon them to be true? There's only one thing that keeps a man from benefiting from the promises of God: that is his refusal to reckon on them. Like a check made out to you: before you get the benefit, you've got to endorse it. Refuse to endorse the check, it's useless, so much paper, no matter how much its maker may have in the bank.

A check is a man's promise to pay. It depends entirely on the signer's name, his integrity, his word. When you have confidence in a man you take his check as readily as cash. If you need money, you simply endorse it. Nothing complicated about that. Minute you endorse it, the maker's resources are available!

The Bible is full of tremendous promises God has made. Back of these is God's name, God's integrity, God's resources. His word is His bond! They are like checks made out to you, bearing God's signature, with the amount left blank for you to fill in. Take any of these promises, fill in the amount of your need, endorse it, and immediately God's promise is operative, God's resources available. If you can reckon on the integrity of a friend to the extent that without questioning you endorse his check and use it as cash, surely you can reckon on God's say so, reckon on His promises!

Got a difficult decision to make, big deal coming up? God can give you wisdom for it! He will, if you reckon on His Word: "If any man lack wisdom, let him ask of God who giveth to all men liberally..." (James 1:5). Got a burden too heavy to bear? Something getting you down? Ruining your efficiency? Clogging your brain with worry? Binding you? "Cast thy burden upon the Lord, and He shall sustain thee..." (Psalm 55:22). Need direction? Money? Strength? Peace of mind? Courage? Poise? Stability? There's a promise from God that covers it! And God stands behind every promise! You can count on Him— implicity!

There was one fellow that carried a $1600 check around in his billfold for eight months. It did him no good! Another died of malnutrition! In his pocket were three checks worth nearly $1000. "Ridiculous!" you say.

You've got a Bible filled with incredibly precious provisions for every need in your life. Ever use it?

§ *YOU CAN KNOW GOD*

*T*here are two classes of men so far as a knowledge of God is concerned: Those men to whom God is an idea, which they are for or against; those men to whom God is a fact in experience! To the first, God is sort of a theory, an abstraction. To to the second He is a reality, part of daily experience, contemporary. They know Him, love Him, serve Him. He is like a friend—real! It's the difference between knowing the facts about someone and knowing him. Here lies the unique essence of the Christian faith. To the Christian man God is an experience not merely an idea.

Rightly understood that's the general difference between the Old and New Testament economy. Not that they are in conflict or opposition but the revelation of God is a growing thing—progressive. In the Old Testament God reveals Himself through words and ideas. In the New Testament God reveals Himself in a Person. "The Word became flesh and dwelt among us…" (John 1:14). The only adequate representation of a personality is a person; ideas about a person never suffice. The Old Testament prophets prepared the way for the New Testament Person. The Old Testament moved up and into the full and complete revelation of the New Testament.

In Jesus Christ God revealed His whole Self as a living Personality. In Christ God invaded human affairs. He walked among men. He identified Himself with them. He demonstrated His concern, His interest, His love! God became real, tangible, personal. Now when a man wants to know what God is like he has but to look at Jesus Christ. The Christian man discovers to his eternal blessing that as he comes to know Jesus Christ, he comes to know God personally, warmly, really!

Strictly speaking, Jesus Christ came not as a teacher or a religionist but as a Savior. He came to redeem men from the curse and penalty of sin. He came to die on a cross. He took on Himself man's condemnation. But the cross was not the end! He rose from the dead! He's alive today—vibrantly alive! Millions of men testify to this! That's the point …the practical, down-to-earth, workable point of the Gospel. God is real. He is seeking to come into a man's life, to live there to bless, strengthen and guide.

You can know God this way! Confess your need. Open your heart. Christ will come in. You'll know God is there—in Christ—in you!

"God, who at sundry times and in divers manners spake in times past unto the father by the prophets, hath in these last days spoken unto us by His Son…" (Hebrews 1:1, 2).

§ FAITH IN GOD OR HIS GIFTS

Sometimes God withdraws His blessings in order to bring us to Himself! Tending to trust Him, love Him, obey Him for the sake of His gifts, our devotion to Him grows in inverse ratio to our preoccupation with His blessings. We have become very "commercial" in our attitude. Faith degenerates into a means of getting what we want. God is treated like a "jolly Santa Claus" or a blessing machine. We "mobilize God for our own purposes." And we grumble and gripe when things fail to go our way. Our faith is strong when circumstances are right, but it takes a nose dive when circumstances are reversed. In adversity we whine! Christian experience is like a roller coaster…up and down, up and down. Because our faith is in the gift rather than the giver!

God must dispossess us of this misplaced trust so He deliberately withdraws the blessing to drive us to Himself. Reaching his extremity is often the only way man will allow God opportunity to prove His faithfulness and integrity. We need the whine knocked out of us. We need to grow up! Genuine faith is rooted and grounded in God Himself —in His eternal, unchangeable, irrevocable integrity! God's faithfulness is the basis of faith! Circumstances may change, but He is changeless! A man may feel depressed and without hope, but God is not affected by man's condition. "He is the same yesterday, today and forever!"

Faith does not allow circumstances to make a liar of God! Nor does it allow man's feelings to impugn God's integrity. Heaven and earth may pass away but His Word stands utterly reliable and dependable, totally trustworthy. Back of God's Word is His unimpeachable character! Faith says with Job, "Though He slay me, yet will I trust Him."

"Let God be true and every man be false…" wrote the Apostle Paul.

§ HOW TO BE A MAN

No man is really himself, his full self, until he is ruled by God! Man will be governed either by God—or a tyrant! The tyrants of money, of power, of prestige, of influence, of popularity or of self (the worse tyrant of all) will possess and dominate the man who does not submit to God's rule. All tyrants enslave the man; only God liberates! Tyrants turn a man in on himself; God turns him out, lets him unfold and grow. The man who is ruled by God is master of everything. The man who refuses to be ruled by God is mastered by everything!

The basic distinction between man and animal, the thing that makes them different, is the vertical in the life of man—the God-man relationship! Man not only has a soul which is the seat of his self-consciousness, but man has a spirit, the seat of God-consciousness! Man (in whom this vertical, this God-consciousness is absent or neglected) is man failing to enjoy the full potential of his life. Man not in touch with God is sometimes less than man! He is subhuman! Man living for something less than God and His glory is man running on half his cylinders—half efficient and half productive. Such a man is not beginning to exploit the possibilities in himself. His utility is wasted!

No other goal but the glory of God will draw the best out of a man. No other goal will demand the limits of a man's intellectual, inventive, productive ability. All other goals leave much lacking, much of man's potential unused. Because God made man for fellowship with Himself—and man is never himself until he enjoys this fellowship as the central reality in his life—man is never true to his nature with God left out!

Friendship with God is the native climate for a man. This is home to him. And when this is missing, man is somehow lost! Man without God at the center is man out of touch. He is like a wheel without a hub, like a compass without a magnetic north. Only when he is right with God is man truly orientated. This is not something to quibble about. You try putting God at the center of your plans. Make room for Him in everything. Take time to read the Bible, to pray and to attend worship. Give God a chance. He will prove Himself. It's the most practical move you can make!

"Seek ye first the kingdom of God, and His righteousness..." (Matthew 6:33).

§ CHRISTIAN PERFECTION

*C*hristian perfection is essentially a personal relationship! We are inclined to think of it in terms of personal piety or strong theological conviction...but these are not the measure of it. Growing up spiritually means increasing insight into the *Person* of Jesus Christ! Not necessarily knowing more about Him, more facts, more theology, but knowing Jesus Himself. (There are those who know very little about Jesus who are deeply devoted to Him. They are theologically uninformed, but personally committed.) One may acquire facts about a personality without contact. Books yield much knowledge about men, but you never get to know the man from books.

It's the personal contact that counts! Many of us know a great deal about the President, but that's a far cry from being on intimate terms with him. There are those who know almost all there is to be known about Jesus: the facts of His life, the dogmas that have collected around Him; but unfortunately Jesus Himself is a stranger to them. And that man who is not personally related to Christ, and growing in this personal relationship, remains a spiritual adolescent to say the least, no matter how much knowledge about Jesus he may have been able to accumulate.

There are some very ugly people who know a lot of theology! This is not uncommon: men, passionately religious, full of pride, bigotry, covetousness, deceit. Some of history's worst scandals were perpetrated by very religious men. The crucifixion of Jesus is a glaring case in point! Pious men can be devils!

Which is more satisfying and constructive—to study the facts about an attractive, worthwhile person...or to spend time with him? Consciously, or unconsciously, we tend to conform to the likeness of the man we respect and admire. The more time we spend with him, the more like him we become. To know Jesus personally, to increase our personal acquaintance and intimacy with Him, is to grow up spiritually! This is authentic maturity!

"But we all, with open face beholding as in a glass the glory of the Lord, are changed into the same image from glory to glory, even as by the Spirit of the Lord" (II Corinthians 3:18).

§ *FOR OR AGAINST?*

*B*oil it down to the real issue: either you believe Jesus or you go along with His enemies! That's putting it on the line, but a man ought to level with himself in this matter. No man is more self-deluded than the one who has found a neat compromise on Jesus. Fuzzy thinking about God comes so easily, if a man bothers to think at all, and a mental jolt helps to get him on balance spiritually.

Complacency is exceedingly subtle when it comes to a man's attitude toward Jesus. Comfortable in his position, he tends to reject automatically anything that disturbs the status quo; his mental reflexes register negative. Thinking is hard work, so he coasts intellectually, occasionally reorganizing his prejudices, thinks he's thinking and relaxes. With the inevitable result that he becomes a bigot and calls it conviction; or an intellectual jellyfish and calls it tolerance. But whatever he calls it, the point is that he's lining up with the worst scoundrels of history when he takes a stand against Jesus. Either a man is for Jesus, or against Him, and there is no middle ground, much as selfish men would like to compromise. What reasonable explanation is there for rejection of Jesus? Why should anyone turn against a perfect Man, and go along with the crowd that liquidated Him?

Three classes of men had a part in His crucifixion: those who engineered it; those who yielded to their pressure; and those who just didn't care. The men who let it happen were as culpable as those who made it happen. Indifference to Jesus Christ not only constitutes rejection of Him and support of His opposition, but involves the loss of eternal benefits which God offers. It is, in fact, rejection of the Father.

Jesus said, "If God were your Father, you would love Me..." (John 8:42).

§ *THE ACID OF INDIFFERENCE*

*W*ho crucified Jesus Christ? The answer is exceedingly illuminating, especially when you reverse the question: "Who did not crucify Him?" It was not the rabble, the disreputable crowd that abounds in every generation. It was not the prostitutes, the quislings, the shysters, the criminals.

Dr. James Stewart of Scotland suggests three forces which put Jesus Christ on the cross: First, the religious force. The greatest hostility to Jesus came from the religionists. Early in His ministry they concocted their conspiracy to discredit Him. Utterly frustrated in their attempts, every one of which backfired, they plotted His liquidation. Records Dr. Luke, "The chief priests and the scribes and the principal men of the people sought to destroy Him...."

Times have not changed. Religion still opposes Jesus Christ!

Second, the political force. Pilate knew Jesus was innocent, but political expediency overruled his conscience. He was the product of his day. Rome had begun to operate on "peace-at-any-price" terms. It was quite logical to sacrifice goodness and justice in the interests of peace.

But these two forces could not have accomplished their insidious deed had it not been for the third force: the indifferent multitude. The respectable people who couldn't care less! The same crowd that tried to make Him king on Palm Sunday cried, "Crucify Him!" five days later. Indifferent men were a tool in the hands of a vicious minority.

Which is always the case: inadvertently, unknowingly, perhaps, but inevitably, the indifferent man plays into the hands of the enemies of righteousness. He is always vulnerable to the diabolical exploitation of evil. He was then. He is today, in the twentieth century! God save us from the terrible degenerative corrosion of indifference!

Jesus said, "He that is not for Me is against Me!"

§ HOW DO YOU LOOK AT SIN?

*O*ne thing that distinguishes a spiritual man is his attitude toward sin. He is not sinless, but he abhors sin, especially in himself. He is not critical of sin in others because he is conscious of the evil potential within himself. He is continually aware of his need of God's forgiveness and mercy. He suffers no illusion about his own imperfections. In fact, if you really want to know what sin is like, read the journal of any saint. You'll never learn about sin from sinners or hypocrites because sin hardens a man and renders him insensitive to its nature and strategy.

The truly spiritual man is sensitive to sin, and is more easily brought under conviction, more readily sorry for his sin, more quickly repentant. What bothers him most about sin is that it is against God! This does not concern the unregenerate man. To be sure sin bothers him, but only because he is afraid of the consequences. Greatest deterrent to sin in the non-spiritual man is fear of being found out. It does not occur to him that sin is an offense against God. At best he thinks of it only in terms of its effect on his fellowman. He recognizes sin as a breach in the man-to-man relationship, but he's totally oblivious to the effect of sin on God. His highest motive for refusing to sin is his concern for others—family, friends, colleagues, or society in general. But most often he resists temptation because he desires acceptance.

The spiritual man abhors sin because it offends God; because it grieves the Holy Spirit of God; because it is like driving fresh nails into the hands and feet of Jesus. He is not indifferent to the effect of his sin on his fellowman, but the terrible thing about sin is its transgression of God's law, its failure to come up to God's standard. Even if he can sin without being discovered by others, he knows that God knows and his desire to please God is preeminent.

"Against Thee and Thee only, have I sinned, and done this evil..." (Psalm 51:4).

§ PROVE THE PROMISES

*G*ot some burden too heavy to carry alone today? Is there some special need in your life—in your home, at the office, on the job, among your friends, in your own heart? Are you facing some big decision that's got you down? Is something coming up in a few days that you don't feel you're prepared to meet? Is something bothering you and you don't even know what it is? You just feel depressed, discouraged, washed out?

Take a moment to consider some of the tremendous promises of God for you! Promises designed to carry you over the rough places. Promises you can depend on! There's not a need in your life, not a problem, difficulty—whether temporal or spiritual—for which the Lord is not more than sufficient. God delights in helping men who will acknowledge their need and come to Him for help. That's the key: some of us are proud, so secular in attitude, that we get the idea it is weak to call on God. Why, the greatest men the world has ever produced knew the wisdom of calling on God in time of need.

Think of Lincoln kneeling alone at his desk in Washington under the unprecedented weight of a nation torn by civil war. Let Lincoln speak to you this morning. He'll tell you that he found unbelievable strength there on his knees. Strength and wisdom for an impossible task. God helped Lincoln. He'll help you. It's not weak to call on the Lord. That's the sign of real manhood. Only hulking bullies won't admit their need, hide their fear by bragging. It's sheer, stupid, immature pride for a man to feel he has to fight battles alone—without God.

Do you need wisdom? "If any man lack wisdom let him ask of God who gives to all men generously and without reproach, and it will be given him" (James 1:5); "Commit thy works to the Lord, and thy thoughts shall be established" (Proverbs 16:3).

Need strength? "The Lord is the strength of my life, of whom shall I be afraid?" (Psalm 27:1); "I can do all things through Christ who strengtheneth me" (Philippians 4:13).

Burdened with some heavy load, some difficulty, some depressing weight in your heart? "Cast thy burden upon the Lord, and He shall sustain thee" (Psalm 55:22).

Perhaps money matters are getting you down. Worried about finances? "My God shall supply all your need according to His riches in glory by Christ Jesus" (Philippians 4:19).

Is there come forthcoming problem bothering you? Some future difficulty eating at you now? "Commit thy way (future) unto the Lord, trust also in Him, and He shall bring it to pass (work it out)" (Psalm 37:5).

"The steps of a good man are ordered by the Lord" (Psalm 37:23).

§ *FAITH IN GOD—OR CIRCUMSTANCES?*

*Y*ou can be the master of your circumstances instead of being at their mercy! The Christian man need never be "under the circumstances." He can always be on top of them! Difficulties make some men; ruin others! It is all in the way a man looks at it, the way he takes it! Not what happens to you, *but how you take what happens* that counts!

It is easy to trust God when things go well. But when you analyze that sort of thing you realize it is not trust in God at all, it is trust in circumstances. All men have "fair-weather" faith that works when things are favorable. But this is not faith in God. This is faith in things as they are! Obviously such faith collapses with reverses!

Christian faith—the faith that counts—is that which depends on God no matter what circumstances are like. This is faith in God Himself, faith in God's character, faith in God's integrity! Working faith! This faith recognizes that God does not change. Circumstances may; God does not! He is "the same yesterday, today, and forever." He can always be depended upon. He is never the victim of circumstances. He is the Lord of circumstances!

Some men let circumstances make a liar of God. They believe God as long as there are no set-backs. But let things turn bad for them, and they act as though God were dead or had no control over circumstances or had forgotten or didn't know what to do. This is not the God of the Bible! This is not the God of the Christian! The God in whom we trust orders circumstances according to His perfect will and purpose! He is never taken by surprise, never caught unawares, never overwhelmed! He is in control every split second! And He will never allow a situation to touch your life that is not designed to make a better man of you. Nothing happens to the Christian man but what God lets happen. And God lets nothing happen but for your growth, your maturity and strength!

Every difficulty, every set-back, every reversal, every disappointment and defeat is ordered by God. It is part of His plan and process whereby the man becomes everything he ought to be. Do not be guilty of the whine and whimper. Remember the God in whom you trust never makes a mistake, never lets a mistake happen to you. Through difficulty become more than a conqueror!

"All things work together for good to them that love God; to them that are called according to His purpose" (Romans 8:28).

§ *YOU'RE NEEDED WHERE YOU ARE*

*H*ave your ever seriously considered the thought that in the economy of God you are indispensable where you are now? God has placed you where you are as an outlet for His grace. That's God's method: Christian men, available, usable as distributors of the Divine resources. God risks His plan with you where you are!

That's the way it began in Acts. The early dynamic spread of the Gospel was the work largely of laymen. They took the message "everywhere." This was the pattern Christ Himself instituted—the pattern of laymen infiltrating into every phase of life, working like "salt" into the very substance of society and business. The Apostle Paul describes the Church of Jesus Christ as a Body: Christ Himself the Head; each Christian a member. Each member has a unique function in the Body. The Body needs each member. One cannot take the place of another. Each is indispensable!

One of the last things Christ did was command His disciples to go everywhere—"into all the world"—taking the Gospel "to every creature." That commission is fulfilled only when each Christian functions in his own world where God has placed Him. It certainly was never Christ's intention that this job should be handled by a relatively few "professional" ministers, evangelists, and missionaries, any more than it is the policy of big business to let a few sales managers do the selling while the salesmen are idle. You'd never get wide distribution that way.

There's a little world around you. It's your world! If you're a Christian man, that world is your responsibility. No one else can touch it. If you fail there, God has no alternate, no substitute. You fail and God's inexhaustible resources are shut out from your world! Preoccupation may be your greatest enemy! It's the excuse of many men! *If things were different here. If I only had the advantages the other fellow has. When I get these other things lined up I'll be free to do God's work.* No, you won't. If you're not doing it now, where you are, you'll not do it later. Preoccupation is sin! Thing to do is to be occupied now with your obligation as a Christian witness.

"Never allow the thought I am of no use where I am...you certainly are of no use where you are not" (Oswald Chambers).

Discipleship begins now, right where you are! "You are my witnesses!" said Jesus Christ.

§ *INTOLERANCE*

Somebody ought to write a book entitled *The Case for Intolerance.* We've pushed tolerance so far that right has been shoved completely out of our lives. There are no real standards anymore in the home, business, the social circle. Anything goes! Tolerance is king! Tolerance has become a little god to us. Broadmindedness has become the chief virtue. And all the starch has gone out of our character. We're like a dish of jelly! It might be well to remember that broad minds like broad rivers are sometimes quite shallow.

Actually tolerance in most cases is really indifference! People who have no serious convictions about anything are not challenged by the convictions of others. It's not a virtue to be tolerant of another's convictions when you have none yourself. That's not tolerance; that's pure laziness! Tolerance gives plenty of people an excuse not to think for themselves. It takes energy to think! It's much easier just to be tolerant. Such people never have convictions, just opinions.

Tolerance has become loose, careless, indifferent to most issues. It gives birth to the "what's-the-difference" attitude. No such thing as right! Sheer subjectivism! Anything a man does is okay...just so he's sincere. What sentimental mouthwash that is! Tolerance as such can be the arch-enemy of a community or nation. It has become that, in fact, in many cases. It is a serious sinister evil and ought to be fought to the death in each of our lives. It waters down everything until there's nothing worthwhile left.

Someone has said, "If we don't stand for something, we'll fall for anything." How true! We're suckers for any silly idea that comes along when we have no serious convictions. Many of us are right at that point so far as religion and morality goes. And while we go along our merry, spineless, careless, indifferent way, Communism, burning with conviction and utterly intolerant of anything that stands in its way, sweeps across the world like a raging tempest!

America needs a good healthy dose of intolerance these days. Intolerance against lies, against immorality, irreligion, prejudice. Intolerance against the subtle secularistic attitude that is eating out the vital center of our lives. Intolerance against that which destroys the best and finest. We need a flash point in our natures that will explode when wrong is done. Christian men who dare not to laugh at stupid, filthy obscenity. Men who have enough "guts" to get mad at sin! Men who realize that tolerating some things is appeasement in its worst form—deadly, destructive appeasement!

"And making a whip of cords, Jesus drove them all, with the sheep and oxen, out of the temple; and He poured out the coins of the money-changers and overturned their tables" (John 2:15).

§ BELIEF IS BASIC

*O*f course belief matters! It makes all the difference in the world. It's the difference between a true American and a milk-sop, jelly-fish of a man. "Men who don't stand for something, fall for anything."

You better make sure the druggist has rather strong convictions about the laws of chemistry before you take your doctor's prescription to him.

You wouldn't waste a plug nickel on a paper edited by a man who has no regard for truth. You want your editor to believe something—and stand up for it!

Take a look at your country! The men who started it believed something! They believed it with a passion that burned like wildfire in their hearts. Their beliefs were the foundation stones of America.

How long has it been since you read the Constitution? That was written by men who believed something. Read it! Read the Declaration of Independence, the Bill of Rights! It will put fire in your blood! They believed something in those days and their belief carved America!

This is a war of belief. Make sure of that! Belief is the bottom issue in this whole tragic mess. Those "Commies" believe something; it's not nice, but they'll die for it! That's what makes them such nasty, fanatical, demoniac enemies.

To believe in God and His Son, Christ, and Truth and Right. That's American, American to the core! The only rag of hope we have in this desperate day is in the men who really believe something. We're lost if we persist in the stupid, unrealistic attitude: it doesn't make any difference what a man believes.

We had better examine our beliefs. A man's a liability in America today if his beliefs are wrong.

"As a man thinketh in his heart, so is he" (Proverbs 23:7).

§ THE CROSS OF CHRIST

When you really think about it and take it seriously, the cross of Jesus is the most enigmatic fact of history! It defies explanation on any reasonable grounds.

Jesus was human in every sense of the word: subject to all the weariness, privation, temptation...yet never giving in, never yielding. He was human nature at its outside best. History records no trace of weakness, sin or selfishness in Him. He epitomized virtue. He was honesty, selflessness, goodness incarnate! He literally spent Himself for others ...never accumulated a thing, never indulged a moment satisfying selfish desires or ambitions. He was a perfect man. Yet men put Him on a cross! To the everlasting shame of humanity it let the only perfect representative of itself be crucified as a common criminal.

The cross was the most despised form of capital punishment. It was so terrible that a Roman citizen could not be crucified, no matter what his crime. It was reserved for the worst offenders—crime's worst penalty! His fanatical enemies were forced to employ false witnesses. Their case fell apart. Pilate could find "no fault in Him." He said Christ was a "just person." Yet he let Him be crucified. Pilate was insufferably weak. What explanation do you make of the cross? What sense is there to it? It is utterly unreasonable, inexplicable by all men's standards. It makes sense only in the light of Divine wisdom—God's plan of redemption.

What made crucifixion so horrible was that it meant death from sheer exhaustion, body dehydration. Normally it took several days. Christ was on the cross only a few hours. Roman guards were staggered by the suddenness of His death. What killed Him? Why did He die so soon? The cross didn't kill Him! He wasn't on it long enough! When you comprehend the death of Jesus, you have the key of the whole plan of God for the salvation of humanity. The cross is the clue, the core, the crux of it! In his impatience Pilate said, "Do you not know that I have power to release you, or power to crucify you?" Christ answered, "You have not power over Me at all...." Another time He said, "No one takes My life from Me. I lay it down of My own accord. I have power to lay it down and power to take it up again."

They didn't take His life from Him. Nothing they could have done would have accomplished that! "In Him was life." He was the author —the source of life! That's why they couldn't keep Him in a tomb! He laid down His life! By the sheer act of His will, He gave up His life! He cried out, "Finished!" What was finished? The thing He had come to do! He came to die on a cross. He was "the Lamb of God" to take away the sin of the world. He laid down His life for you, for me, for all men.

"Without the shedding of blood is no remission of sin" (Hebrews 9:22); "The blood of Jesus Christ, God's Son, cleanseth us from all sin" (I John 1:7).

§ *THE MIGHT-HAVE-BEEN*

*O*ne of the saddest spectacles in life is the "might-have-been"...the young man who started with unlimited possibilities who petered out in the long pull. There's nothing more pitiful, more pathetic, than these tremendous young men who began in a brilliant flash, then fizzled out. They had a glorious future ahead. Their lives could have been immeasurably productive, creative, constructive. They might have been the future giants of business and industry. They might have filled a desperate need in these uncertain times. But they couldn't take it, couldn't stand success. It went to their heads. They began to wander, lose their spiritual anchor, drift, blend into the status quo, conform. Being "somebody" became more important than being Godly.

Some men grow with success. Others just swell. Prestige, position, recognition cause some men to season and mature. Others just seem to ferment and spoil. They get heady, frothy, empty. Some men mellow with success. Others rot.

The leadership of strong young men, big men, dependable men, is desperately needed today. Men who know how to keep their feet on the ground; who have stability; who are solid, realistic, Christians! We need men who humble themselves before God and recognize that all they have, all they are is because of God's grace and goodness. Men who refuse to exalt themselves and exalt the Lord. Men who will never sacrifice principle for position, who are Christ-like, Godly. Men who have the Christian perspective!

Do you know a young fellow who is becoming a "might-have-been"? Get next to him! Help him see himself, get squared away with himself—and God! Stop him before it is too late. Before he leaves behind him a tragic trail of things that might have been had he been the man he should be—a trail of broken hearts, shattered hopes, disillusioned friends. The world can't afford "might-have-beens" now! Time is running out. It's late!

And about you, yourself! Are you all you ought to be? You're needed, too. Needed on God's side. Stand up and be counted!

"Thus saith the Lord, Let not the wise man glory in his wisdom, neither let the mighty man glory in his might, let not the rich man glory in his riches: but let him that glorieth glory in this, that he understandeth and knoweth Me, that I am the Lord..." (Jeremiah 9:23, 24).

§ JUST GOOD—OR THE BEST?

*G*ood things can be your greatest enemy! Good things can hinder your effectiveness as much, or more, than bad things! Your most consistent choices lie between the good and the best! The good is often, too often, the enemy of the best!

You are too wise to be coerced by bad things in the normal course of events. You won't be misled by the obvious. But you may let good things chip away at your time and energy until they are used up with nothing accomplished. The intelligent man does not do a thing just because it isn't wrong. His choice is governed by more mature standards than just right and wrong. The wise man has to be selective about his time. He must choose among many good things that which is best. Someone has said you can tell a wise man by the way he uses his wastebasket.

There are plenty of "average" men who seldom do a wrong thing... and they seldom do anything else! They're good, but good for what? Good for nothing! Just neutral, average men. Henry L. Doherty, the great industrialist, said, "I can hire men to do everything but two things, think, and do things in the order of their importance." There's the difference between the man who goes to the top and the fellow who is busy getting nowhere. One keeps busy just avoiding wrong things; the other utilizes his time with the best. It has been said that if a minister says he has a good golf score, he is either lying or neglecting his work. Maybe that's true of some businessmen too. Nothing wrong with golf, but it makes some men neglect more important things.

It's pitiful to hear a man argue about a thing he wants to do: "I don't see any harm in it!" Perhaps not! But what's it doing for him? Does it make him a better man? Actually this kind of man is filling his life with piddly little things that do not harm...and they do nothing else! Tragic little men never get very far, always stay pretty close to bottom! Time is precious. No man can afford to waste it. Wise men refuse to throw it away. They organize their time, make it count for the most. They are not the slaves of time; they are its masters!

"See then that ye walk circumspectly, not as fools, but as wise, redeeming the time, because the days are evil" (Ephesians 5:15, 16).

§ *DON'T DISTURB, GOD!*

*L*eaving the hotel room to attend church one Sunday morning, I passed door after door along the corridor on which a familiar little card had been hung over the door knob. The card bore a simple request: "PLEASE DO NOT DISTURB." America was sleeping in on Sunday morning!

Reminded me of a prayer I read in the magazine *The Christian Evangelist.* "Almighty God, as I lie here on the sofa this lovely Sunday morning, surrounded by the Sunday paper, and half listening to one of the big preachers over the radio, it has just come to me that I have lied to Thee and to myself. I said I did not feel well enough to go to church. That was not true! I was not ambitious enough! I would have gone to my office had it been Monday morning. I would have played golf had it been Wednesday afternoon. I would have attended my luncheon club had it been this noon. I would have been able to go to a picture show if it had been Friday night. But it is Sunday morning, and Sunday illness covers a multitude of sins. God have mercy on me! I have lied to Thee and to myself. I was not ill...I am lazy and indifferent!"

Please do not disturb, God.

How many of us have this sign hanging over the door of our heart? There is a man who quit going to church when he reached junior high age. Do you know what his reason was for quitting? Sunday after Sunday he was sent off to Sunday school as a child while his father remained at home. He began to look forward to the day when he could be a man like his dad and not have to go to church. He grew up with the idea that church-going was not manly. He admired, respected and loved his dad...and his dad never went to church.

He wanted to be like his dad!

Your son wants to grow up to be like you! You're his standard for manliness, for greatness. You're his measure of success!

"And let us consider one another to provoke unto love and to good works; not forsaking the assembling of ourselves together..." (Hebrews 10:24, 25).

§ THE FADE-OUT

*A*re you trying to live on memories? This can be devastating spiritually!

The man who must rely on past experience for present strength stands on the edge of spiritual peril. Pity him whose only inner resources are warmed-over blessings! He is in danger of becoming a sentimentalist. Sentimentalism cools and gels into complacency and indifference, and/or counterfeit piety.

Lack of spiritual reality and vitality indicates disobedience! Somewhere along the line there was something the man was unwilling to do or something he did that he should not have done. Disobedience blocks the flow of blessing!

A man may think he's getting away with it, but he pays an awful price in the long run. Christ becomes unreal; faith stagnates; love for God (and man) grows cold. Professionalism sets in, deadens spiritual perception, sensitivity and response.

The solution is confession—honest, frank, humble confession to God. (Remember the blood of Christ cannot cleanse excuses. It only cleanses sin!) Once a man confesses to God, he is in a position to receive Divine forgiveness through faith in God's Word and surrender to Christ! It doesn't take God long to restore the bloom and fragrance to a man's spirit, providing the man is willing to confess his sin, turn from it, and commit his way to the Lord!

Bring your Christian experience up-to-date!

"If we confess our sins, He is faithful and just to forgive us our sin and to cleanse us from all unrighteousness" (I John 1:9); "If we walk in the light as He is in the light, we have fellowship with one another, and the blood of Jesus Christ, God's Son, cleanseth us from all sin" (I John 1:7).

§ THE STRATEGY OF CONCENTRATION

*H*ave you ever noticed how much easier it is to learn your way around in a strange city when you're driving the car? Much easier than when you're a passenger and someone else is driving. You remember street names and numbers and directions with ease; whereas when you're a passenger you can go over the same route many times without ever becoming familiar with it. The reason is quite obvious— and simple. The driver of the car is paying strict attention to the route and the landmarks. The passenger has his mind on other things, lets the driver take the responsibility.

Or you've noticed how in a group of people one can be completely out of touch with the conversation although outwardly he seems to be paying attention to it. Truth of the matter is that the man, though seeming to look and listen, is mentally "wool gathering." He's somewhere else in his thoughts. This can be true between two people. One is speaking and the other seems to be listening, but actually he's a million miles away in his thinking...and the speaker isn't getting through to him at all! Perhaps you've been on the talking end of this disconcerting experience. Fellow looking straight at you but you feel he's missing everything you're saying. You feel he's not with you; he's not really getting it! Nothing unusual about this: It's common even among friends. And the explanation is simple: A man sees or hears or feels what he focuses his attention on! He can be surrounded by a crowd and all the time his consciousness is centered on something else: A problem at home or in the office, a favorite mountain trout stream, a tricky hole at the golf course, a business deal. The conversation swirls around him, out of focus, at the edge of his consciousness, and he's barely aware of it.

This natural ability of the mind to get a "fix" on something is the secret to one of the wisest strategies in the Christian life. This is the key to the walk of faith in the midst of turmoil, confusion, pressure! Practicing God-consciousness every day is the master plan for poise and balance and precision in the life. It isn't easy! It takes discipline! A thousand distractions will drag the mind away from God! But it pays off! Pays off in efficiency, in sanity, in inward strength, in perspective! This practice gets a man on top of the load; enables him to walk in the midst of the fuss of life under control.

One man began by thinking about God for thirty minutes each day. It was tough at first, but he got on to it. Another tries to think God-ward at least an hour. Another does it every time he remembers. One does it as he drives to work and returns home. One does it by memorizing Scripture passages. One man gets to his office thirty minutes early; spends the time with God. Another takes a short walk and centers his attention on God. Try it!

"For the weapons of our warfare are not worldly but have divine power to destroy strongholds. We destroy every proud obstacle to the knowledge of God, and take every thought captive to obey Christ" (II Corinthians 10:4, 5).

§ *STUMBLING BLOCKS OR STEPPING STONES*

*I*t's not what happens to you, but how you react to what happens to you that really counts in the long run! All men have difficulties! In one way or another tragedy, sorrow, disappointment, failure come to every man. No one escapes them. They are part of life. But they make, or mar, a man, depending on how he takes them and how he reacts to them. Trouble makes fiends of some men; saints of others!

Some men take every problem, every failure, as final. They are over-powered by it and driven to despair. Other men take problems as a part of their education, a means to an end like a runner takes a hurdle, just part of the race. To some, troubles are catastrophes that disrupt, dismay, discourage, defeat. They are taken as interruptions and are allowed to confuse a man, getting him off balance, out of pitch, disorganized. To others, every difficulty is an opportunity to learn, to grow, to mature and mellow. They take trouble in their stride, as part of life, to be expected and mastered! They don't give in to trouble and yield in weak acquiescence, they utilize it, make it count for blessing. They use it as a stepping stone, not as a stumbling block.

Troubles can't get you down unless you let them! You yourself determine whether they shall turn to triumph or tragedy! See in trouble an undesirable hindrance, unfortunate circumstance; in all probability it will get you down, debilitate you, frustrate you. See in trouble one of the many unexpected variables in life, an incident that can turn to your advantage, to be taken in course, accepted and mastered; it will strengthen you and sharpen you.

The Christian man, the truly Christian man, sees in trouble a counter-balance for life. It is not meant to weigh him down, drag him under. Trouble gives balance, poise, tensile strength. He takes life as it comes from God, incident by incident, minute by minute. He is not embittered by adversity; he learns to thank God for it and to see in it hidden blessing. Christian character cannot be imputed. It must be developed! It is developed by exercise. It is exercised by adversity!

"Count it all joy when you meet various trials, for you know that the testing of your faith produces stedfastness" (James 1:2, 3) [RSV]).

§ *MATURITY*

*T*hree stages in man's growth: First, helpless infancy—completely dependent; second, cocky adolescence—completely independent; third, mature manhood—interdependent.

Unfortunately some adults never grow up, never move out of the adolescent age. Remaining cockily independent, they fail (like the adolescent) to recognize their need of those about them: family, friends, colleagues. Mastered by his ego, the adolescent adult is under the illusion that he is "self-made" and therefore solely responsible for his attainments. Nobody dictates to him about anything! He is his own master, and he usually lets the world know it! ("I do as I please!") His immaturity is showing!

Worst of all is his independence from God...

Totally unaware that "every good and perfect gift is from above"—that "a man can receive nothing except it be given him from heaven"—that life itself is a gift (which he had nothing whatever to do with getting)—he acts as though he is a self-generated, self-sustained being. He is a horrible caricature of the authentic independence and self-reliance God intended every man should have.

Man was made free, designed to be independent, the master of the world about him, but his freedom, his independence are God's gift and work only as the man himself is mastered by God. Mastered by God, man is master of himself and his environment. Independent of God, man is mastered by pride and victimized by his environment. Either he is ruled by God or enslaved by tyrants! Man enjoys authentic freedom and independence only when he chooses to be God's servant to do God's will.

The most self-reliant, dependable man is the one who relies upon God and lives in dependence upon Him. You are your best when Jesus Christ is your Lord and your daily life is ordered according to His will.

Jesus said, "Without Me, you can do nothing" (John 15:5).

§ *THE ESSENCE OF CHRISTIANITY*

*C*hristianity begins and ends with a Person!

It did not begin with a group of theologians working together to develop a doctrinal system which men were to believe and by which they became Christian. Nor did it begin with the speculation of philosophers. Christianity is not the invention of man's mind. The more one understands the New Testament the more persuaded he becomes that it is uninventable! And it is not an ethical system! Ethics and morals are involved to be sure...but Christianity did not begin with a code of ethics laid down as a "rule of thumb" which men must follow to become Christians.

Christianity began with a Person! A Man utterly unlike any other man who ever lived before Him or followed after Him! He was completely unique! He had no learning by the standards of His day, yet He confounded the scholars with His wisdom. His teaching was the greatest ever spoken by the lips of men. Born in a stable, raised in the humble home of a carpenter, Himself a carpenter by trade, He lived a life that was perfection in flesh! History vindicates Him as the one perfect, sinless Man who ever lived!

His claims for Himself were literally "out of this world." Considering those claims at their face value you either worship this Man, or you label Him a fake or fool. For if what He said of Himself is not true, Jesus Christ was the most deluded egomaniac who ever lived, or He consciously misrepresented Himself in the greatest hoax ever foisted on the human race. If Jesus Christ was not what He claimed to be, He was either a psychotic or a "con-man."

Jesus claimed that obedience to His teaching constituted the only dependable foundation for life: "He that heareth My sayings and does them is a wise man...Whosoever heareth My sayings and does them not is a foolish man...." He claimed that His teaching was final: "Heaven and earth shall pass away but My word shall never pass away!"

He claimed equality with God. This in fact was the ground for His conviction and crucifixion. His enemies accused Him of making this claim. Jesus did not deny it! He could have escaped the horror and ignominy of the cross by simply repudiating His claim. But He did not ...for He could not deny the truth! "I and the Father are one." "He that hath seen Me hath seen the Father."

He claimed that rejection of Himself constituted rejection of God. "He who does not honor the Son does not honor the Father."

He claimed He would rise from the dead...that this in fact would be the supreme evidence supporting all His claims. "One sign shall be given, the sign of the Prophet Jonah...."

What is Jesus Christ to you? Son of God? Savior? Or fake? Fool?

§ MAN AT HIS BEST

Sure a man can get along without God!

Like he can get along without his health. Like he can get along without an arm or a leg, without his sight or his hearing. Of course a man can get along... But he'll never be the man he could be! What kind of a man is it that is willing just to get along? Plenty of men half-broken physically have gotten along in the world. Health hasn't been up to par, but they've managed. They've made a reasonable success of things, enjoyed a reasonable amount of happiness. Life has been adequate...*but not full!* A four-engine airliner can limp along on two or three engines, but what a difference when she's under full power!

What difference does it make whether or not a man takes God seriously? After all isn't religion a "take it or leave it" proposition? It's good for them that want it. It's all right if a man leaves it alone. Is it a convenience—or a necessity?

Three reasons why it is imperative that a man take God seriously! In the first place man is incurably religious. If he doesn't follow the true God, he'll find a substitute. This is inevitable! (Some of the most religious men are atheists. They believe with all their heart in "no god"!) Second, a man becomes like his god! His life forms and fashions itself inexorably after the image of God (or whatever takes the place of God). Though made in the image of God, he grows into the image of his idol! Which means a man who follows a false god is less a man than he could be. He is a might-have-been. He is something less than his potential. Third, man was made for fellowship with God. To be in tune with reality, in harmony with life, he must be in touch with God.

To be out of fellowship with God is to be maladjusted. Life is distorted and twisted. It is to be like a fish out of water, like a bird with clipped wings. The man not right with God is never really right with others and never right with himself. Man out of touch with God is man out of line, out of focus, a caricature of himself. A man is never himself except the Lord is his God!

Man ruled by God is man at his best!

But most significant of all is man's eternal destiny. God has set eternity in our hearts. Three-score-years-and-ten at best leave a man barely touching the edge of life's possibilities. Fulfillment comes only in eternity.

Jesus says, "What shall it profit a man if he gain the whole world and lose his own soul?" (Matthew 16:26).

§ *MEANING*

*H*istory doesn't make sense if you look for meaning inside it! A man will never completely understand the world situation as it is (in fact he'll not even understand himself) until he sees behind the scenes an irreconcilable conflict between two kingdoms: the kingdom of good and the kingdom of evil, the kingdom of God and the kingdom of Satan. History is meaningless—"a tale told by an idiot, full of sound and fury, signifying nothing"—unless seen in the light of this fundamental conflict between righteousness and wickedness.

Back of the tension in the world, underneath the conflict, the pressures and strife, is this inexorable ambition of Satan in his deceptive, insidious strategy to win the world. This spiritual warfare breaks out here and there into physical wars: personal, domestic, industrial, civil or international. But these wars are the symptom of the great unseen warfare. History makes sense; civilization makes sense; a man's personal life makes sense, only in terms of a plan outside history.

Imagine a line one thousand miles long (or a hundred thousand, it makes no difference). Let this line represent eternity. Now imagine a space six inches long marked off on that line. Those six inches represent time from beginning to end. Let a pin point represent our civilization within that history. Look for meaning within that pin point, within that six inches, and you get the idea. History makes sense only in terms of eternity.

Imagine a second line representing a Divine purpose. It begins at the beginning of the thousand-mile line and continues to the end of it. That purpose moves right through the six inches of history, right through the pin point of our civilization. And that Divine purpose gives meaning to the six inches of history, the pin point of our civilization.

God is at work in history. He is beyond history, but He has a purpose which is being worked out through history. It is this purpose of God that makes history make sense. It is God's purpose that makes life make sense! In fact the idea of progress did not exist before the Old Testament. It is from the Bible the concept of progress comes. As someone has put it: History is His story!

The point of course is that each man finds life full of meaning and purpose when he lines up with God's purpose, yields to God's will. And conversely man is frustrated when he refuses God's will and purpose.

"It is God's plan that everything that exists in heaven and earth shall find its perfection and fulfillment in Jesus Christ" (Ephesians 1:10 [Phillips translation]).

§ *WHO HAS THE ANSWER?*

*B*oil it right down. What is more naive than the idea that human nature is going to solve its own problems by its own ingenuity? It is sheer blindness in the light of history and current events—this idea which still perseveres among some enlightened men—that man has it in himself, by his own effort and resources, to build a world of peace. Yet modern oratory is filled with it as though it were a new doctrine, that man has all the answers if he will just try hard enough, long enough, sincerely enough.

What lesson of history is more obvious than this: The total bankruptcy of man's best, the futility of man pulling himself up by his own bootstraps? Our progress (if it may be called that) in science and technology has been accompanied by a corresponding decline in morals and spirituality. As our civilization has developed it has become more corrupt. We are scientific geniuses...and spiritual morons! All brains and no soul! (This is not the word of pessimistic preachers, it is cold, hard fact!) The very progress we boast has become the greatest threat to our suvival! This is the dilemma of intelligent, sophisticated, modern man.

Where do we go from here? What new system to organize or stimulate or motivate or control human nature remains to be tried? He was a wise man who said, "The only lesson history teaches us is that we learn nothing from history." We are faced with the staggering fact that man has unbelievable resources and know-how, yet instead of solutions, his complications increase. Brilliant minds, using the latest technology and science, seek for answers, keep coming up with greater complexities.

How naive can smart people be? Continue to pin our hopes on human schemes to bring us the peace for the which the world languishes ...while we remain utterly indifferent to the Prince of Peace. Put all our eggs in the basket of human resources, and at the same time ridicule or ignore the Gospel of Jesus Christ.

Human nature needs to be tamed...not organized! Man himself is his big dilemma! "We have harnessed the atom," declared General Carlos Romulo, "but we will never make war obsolete until we find a force that will bridle the passions of men and nations." The Gospel of

Jesus Christ is that force! We must try it—or perish!

"...it is the power of God unto salvation..." (Romans 1:16).

§ *TRUE RESPONSIBILITY*

*T*he greater the man, the greater the danger...if he is indifferent to God!

"What is the greatest thought that can occupy a man's mind?" Daniel Webster was asked. "My accountability to God!" was his unhesitating reply. Our twentieth century has seen a demonstration several times over of the inevitable result driven to its logical conclusion when men lose or repudiate their sense of accountability to God. Hitler, Mussolini, Stalin bear striking witness to the horrible mutilation of human character that occurs when men "refuse God in their knowledge."

It is his "vertical" drive or urge or capacity that distinguishes man from animals. It is this freedom of choice with its incumbent responsibility that is the essence of God's image in man. When the responsibility is forsaken, the freedom is repudiated! The process of deterioration takes time...but it is inevitable! Man can get by ignoring his responsibility to God, but the ultimate consequences are inevitable. (This is as true of a nation as it is of the individual.)

Into every human heart God has placed a delicately sensitive instrument called the conscience. This was "built in" as man's contact with God. It was designed as an inner compass to guide him in God's way. When the compass is ignored, or the metal of another allegiance pulls the needle from its "magnetic north," the life is led off course. It may be only a fraction of a degree off course, but as the life progresses the divergence between God's way and the misdirection increases imperceptibly until there is a terrible lostness. Being a delicate instrument the conscience can be easily scarred and impaired. If its needling is ignored long enough, its sharp edge becomes blunt and no longer penetrates a man's consciousness. It is exceedingly vulnerable to indifference or deliberate disobedience. It speaks more and more softly until even its whisper is silenced. Finally a man can go on without ever being disturbed by the conscience.

In the simplest terms this is brainwashing. It neutralizes, then destroys, the conscience. And whether the neutralizing process results from man's indifference, the damage is no less catastrophic in the end.

"And since they did not see fit to acknowledge God, God gave them over to a reprobate mind..." (Romans 1:28).

§ *PERSONAL FAITH*

*D*o you have a personal history with Jesus Christ? Or do you have a second-hand faith?

A man says, "Of course I'm a Christian: I was born in America." Another says, "Sure I'm a Christian; I'm not a Jew!" Or, "What do you think I am, a heathen? Of course I'm a Christian!" Someone else says, "My father was a preacher" or "a deacon" or "an usher" or "a Sunday school teacher." There are those who can boast of a great ancestry in the Church.

But you can't inherit Christianity!

It comes by first-hand experience! In fact, the man who enjoys a rich Christian heritage is so much the more condemned if he has not been induced by such heritage to a personal commitment to Christ. (Knowledge equals responsibility!) Resting on the laurels of past generations, a man damns his own soul! The greater his opportunity to embrace authentic Christianity, the greater his judgment if he neglects it!

Christian faith begins with a first-hand experience of Jesus Christ Himself. The Christian enjoys a personal, living relationship with the Son of God. History is basic to Christian faith, but the fact is that Christ is contemporary. He did not remain in the tomb. He rose from the grave! And every generation since has been confronted by the living Son of God! What a man does today with the living Christ is the vital question! The eternal welfare of his soul, his present personal effectiveness here and now, depend upon this relationship!

Christ confronts you today through His Church: The worship, the Scriptures, the sermon. He confronts you through Christian fellowship, through the witness of the individual Christian. He confronts you through circumstances! In multitudinous ways Christ confronts you daily, seeking your trust and obedience, seeking to give you all that God has offered you for time and eternity. What will you do with Jesus? What is He to you? What place do you give Him in your life?

"He who believes in him is not condemned; he who does not believe is condemned already, because he has not believed in the name of the only Son of God. And this is the judgment, that the light has come into the world, and men loved darkness rather than light because their deeds were evil" (John 3:18, 19 [RSV]).

§ *YOUR INFLUENCE*

*I*t is not just a question of where you go and what you do yourself. It's a question of where you are leading others; how you are influencing those around you. You are somebody's hero you know! You may not realize it (he will never tell you) but he watches you carefully, respects you, studies you, tries to emulate you. Maybe it is your own son! Dad is always the greatest hero to his own boy. Whether consciously or not, he wants to grow up to be like you. He is developing life patterns: a way of thinking, a way of looking at life, evaluating it in terms of what he sees in you!

There comes a time in every lad's life when he stops listening to what Dad says—and watches what Dad does! Here's a boy growing up. Each Sunday morning Mother dresses him in his Sunday-go-to-meeting duds. Off he goes to Sunday school. Dad stays behind in slippers and robe, buried in Sunday papers...or he is out in the yard putting in his weekly stint at the lawn mower or playing a round of golf. And his boy goes reluctantly off to Sunday school, thinking of the day when he is a man like Dad and will not have to go to church. Though he does not realize it, he is getting the idea that church is not for grown-up men—at least not men like his dad!

Subtle? Isn't it? Diabolically subtle! Little boys have big eyes and big ears. They hear and see with an acute, sharp awareness. Their minds delicate, sensitive recording discs, picking up everything.

Most juvenile delinquency begins that way! Being a man to many boys is simply a matter of being able to smoke, drink, play poker, swear, tell a dirty joke. These things are masculine to boys... Where do you think they get the idea that this is manhood? They don't dream it up in a vacuum! They get it watching men, men they admire and respect. Not skid-row men, not gutter snipes, but well-dressed, cultivated, smart men. The classier the man, the more attractive his bad habits to the boy. "Men of Distinction" stuff... Somebody's following you! Where are you leading him?

"Wherefore, if meat make my brother to offend, I will eat no flesh while the world standeth, lest I make my brother to offend" (I Corinthians 8:13).

§ *FINAL VICTORY*

A prayer of the late Peter Marshall while serving as chaplain of the United States Senate suggests a sane and strong perspective for the wise man to take. "Our Father in Heaven, give us the long view of our word and world. Help us to see that it is better to fail in a cause that will ultimately succeed, than to succeed in a cause that will ultimately fail."

There is a pathetic kind of success, success in a cause that is doomed to failure! Yet there are men who line up in this kind of a cause. They take the short view of things, demand the pay-off long before it is due! They may think they are winning, but they deceive only themselves! In the final tally, their success was only delusion, a wisp, a shadow, a fleeting illusion of victory. Men who demand premature settlements of life end up with ashes!

What could be worse? A good man investing his strength, energy, time and money in a cause that simply cannot win in the long run— pinning his hopes to futility, sinking his life into a worthless enterprise! They pushed MacArthur out of Manila, but he came back. The Nipponese won many battles. At times it looked hopeless for the Allied cause. But in the end they won. America lost many battles in Europe in the last World War. But she won the war! That is after all what counts: not just battles, but the war!

This was the great burden of Abraham Lincoln during those bitter years of national schism. He was not concerned whether or not God was on his side. His concern was that *he be on God's side!* Some men try to get God on their side: Their prayers, their gifts, their attendance at worship, their zeal are all designed to win God's approval, designed to get Divine aid for their own projects. This is the caricature of consecration! On the other hand, man on God's side can't lose! He may fail in some of life's battles, but every failure contributes to ultimate success! There will be defeat, but it only serves to sweeten final victory!

It looked like Satan had won at Calvary. That was a black hour. Then came the Resurrection! God took the worst thing Satan could do to His Son—a cross, and turned it into the greatest triumph for God and man—redemption! This is the surest thing in life...*the inevitable triumph of Jesus Christ!* Be wise, man; line up with Him!

"...in all things we are more than conquerors through Him that loved us" (Romans 8:37).

§ *HUMILITY IS STRENGTH*

*Y*ou have it within your power to take the steps, make the choice, which will mean most to your home, your job, your business. Most to yourself. That is the step which turns your life, your work, your home over to God to be run His way, in His strength and by His grace.

Face it, the besetting sin of most of us is pride. It is our worst enemy. It whips most of us daily. It robs us of friends. It comes between husband and wife. It drives rifts between business associates. It is disintegrating, dulling, boring. Not the obvious brand of pride! Not conceit! Most of us are too smart for that! But the subtle, insidious, subversive brand that masquerades as "self sufficiency." The "wolf in sheep's clothing" variety. It is most dangerous because on the surface it sounds so right, so strong, so manly. Everybody respects a man who is big enough to fight his battles, who is able to make his own way. But unmask it and see it for what it is. It is stupid, stuffy, double-damning pride.

The plain fact is nobody makes his own way! "Self-made men" are a misnomer! Every man that ever got anywhere did so with the help of multitudes of others: a mother or a dad, school teachers, friends, associates, helpers, faithful employees...but most of all GOD! And that's the worst thing about that kind of pride. It rules out God. It acts as though God had nothing to do with it at all. That's sheer blindness!

You can't think of a really great man in your experience who is not a humble man. Humility is a basic requirement for greatness. Men love a humble man. They follow him, emulate him. Only little men bloat and swell! Humility was at the bottom of the greatness of Jesus Christ. "He humbled Himself...." And it is at the bottom of all greatness in Americans today, whether in business, the professions, industry or labor.

You personally have everything in the world to gain by humbling yourself before God daily. Admit your need of Him; confess your sin; ask His forgiveness and strength. Gear into God's life. Get the Divine tempo into your blood. "In all thy ways acknowledge Him..." (Proverbs 3:6). Let Jesus Christ into your life. Let Him have your life. You will become the man God wants you to be, the man you most want to be.

"...the great man humbleth himself..." (Isaiah 2:9); "...God opposes the proud but gives grace to the humble.... Humble yourselves before the Lord and He will exalt you" (James 4:6, 10).

§ NEW BIRTH IS NECESSARY

*H*ave you been twice born?

Jesus said a man must—that entrance into the Kingdom of Heaven required a second birth, a new birth. In fact He was quite blunt in declaring that one could not even see the Kingdom unless he was born anew, a condition laid down to a man highly qualified ethically and religiously: Nicodemus, a ruler of the Jews.

Nicodemus was no slouch when it came to religion or morals. He was a good man, an exceedingly good man, who took his religion very seriously. He was a leader of men, outstanding among his people. Everything about Nicodemus was exemplary. He was a solid citizen, way above the average in the basics of life. But Jesus told him that he lacked that which made possible his entrance into the Kingdom of God. His morals and ethics, his civic leadership, his unimpeachable life, his religious sincerity were not adequate. He required the *new birth*.

It takes something more than ethics or religion to get a man into the Kingdom!

A Christian is a twice-born man! He is more than a man striving to live a good life; more than a man doing his best! He is the recipient of the gift of God which is eternal life. He is a man in whom the power of God has done that which only God can do...create! He is one who has been made a new man in Christ, literally the product of the creative work of God! Ethics are involved in this work of God, but they are the result of something far more basic—spirituality.

The Christian lives by a new dimension altogether which was absent from his life until he was regenerated (born anew) by the power of God. This new dimension (vertical and spiritual) is the root of which true ethics and true morality are the fruit. Christian morality has to do with a man's *being* rather than his *doing*; with his nature rather than his deeds. The Christian has a new disposition, a new nature, literally infused into him by the creative act of God through Jesus Christ. Are you a twice born man—a spiritual man, or just a natural man doing his best?

"Ye must be born again!" (John 3:7).

§ *FAILURE IS NOT FINAL*

*A*re you afraid of failure? That is the thought-provoking question asked by John L. Beckley in the title of a brochure he wrote for the General Motors Corporation for distribution to its employees. It is a good question to face squarely! Fear of failure is one of the most debilitating, paralyzing, disintegrating things that can grip a man. It ties him in knots; it cuts efficiency to zero; it makes failure almost inevitable. When a man's afraid of failure he freezes, tries too hard and can't think straight. His fingers become thumbs. He's licked before he starts. If he starts at all! Some men won't even try a thing because they're so afraid of failing. Which is ridiculous. There is certainly no virtue in not failing if one does not try! Failure is not sin. Not to try is!

The plain fact is the men who have gotten places, really produced, accomplished things worthwhile, are the men who have been willing to risk failure over and over again...willing to suffer the humiliation, the ridicule of failure. They kept on...and won! Hundreds could be named, such as Lincoln, Ford, Edison, Pasteur who failed many times. But each time they failed they learned something. Each failure made them better men, more qualified for the success to come. Which is significant! Because to succeed without failure puts a man behind the eight-ball. He hasn't learned the lessons that failure teaches. He hasn't had the benefit of the seasoning, tempering, maturing and mellowing action of failure in his life. Often that kind of success goes to a man's head instead of his heart. He swells rather than grows. He gets too big for his pants, and he is destroyed by success.

Settle it right now: Big men, doing big things, make big mistakes. Little men make little mistakes. Some men don't make mistakes... and they don't make anything else either. The way to whip fear of failure is to see it for what it is! Failure is part of life. It is never final! It is part of learning. A way to grow! Men can step on failure, use it as a stepping stone to better things...or they can stumble on failure, depending on how they take it! Really the most important thing in God's sight is neither success or failure, but how a man plays a game. Win, lose, or draw, the man who does it God's way, the right way, is the victor!

Jesus says, "He that seeks his life will lose it—but he that loses his life for My sake will find it" (Matthew 10:39)..

§ PREPARING FOR THE INEVITABLE

*O*ne difference between the great man and the merely mediocre is *vision*! The big man takes the long look, anticipates exigencies and plans accordingly. This is a clue to accomplishment: preparing for eventualities so that everything doesn't go "down the drain" with reverses. The man with ability to see ahead, around corners, and make decisions that hold water in terms of the future, is the man who goes places!

But strangely, wise and practical as this allowance for emergencies is, there are intelligent, wise men who neglect it in its most important phase! They plan carefully, thoroughly, for emergencies that may never happen...and often are careless about the one thing in life that is inevitable!

Three incidents occurred recently which emphasized the fleeting, transitory, unpredictable nature of life: A large airliner let down in

Chicago, its one stop between Los Angeles and New York. The body of a man who had died in flight was taken off. In his pockets were several thousand dollars, travel folders and tickets. The first leg of his round-the-world journey was the last! It ended in Chicago...23,000 miles short of his plans.

In Southern California an intimate, happy group gathered for dinner. In a way it was a farewell for one, a retired milling executive. In a few days he would be leaving for a long-planned vacation in Europe. As he carved the meat, the sharp knife slipped and plunged into his chest. He was gone in a matter of hours!

Two A.M. Sunday, March 1. Two cars crash sickeningly. Behind one wheel a fine young man slumps crushed. Six hours later he is dead! For weeks he's been getting ready to open his new office. Just starting his practice, he had planned carefully. With pride he put the finishing touches on that Saturday evening. Everything was set for a grand opening on Monday morning. Less than 24 hours later he was gone!

None of them planned it that way! But that's life, man! If there were no way one could insure his eternal welfare, it would be excusable. But eternal security is available to every man who will receive it. Jesus Christ sacrificed His life to provide it for every man. What is wiser than insuring against the inevitable!

"What shall it profit a man if he gain the whole world, and lose his own soul?" (Matthew 16:26); "God so loved the world that He gave His only begotten Son, that whosoever believeth on Him should not perish..." (John 3:16).

§ *ALL CHRISTIANS AGREE ON THIS!*

*R*ecently in the column of a daily newspaper, the writer expressed a point of view which is conspicuous for its utter distortion of the truth. It is strange how an intelligent, normally well-informed columnist could err so thoroughly! Not that he was malicious. He was simply uninformed—or misinformed. He manifested a pitiful ignorance of the Christian Church which men who influence opinion ought to correct. Were it simply an isolated view it could be ignored, but inasmuch as it was held by great masses of people on the basis of which caricature they repudiate Christianity, it should be considered by all thinking people!

Wrote the columnist, quite dogmatically, "...the different denominations are quarreling among themselves, each claiming to have the only road to salvation, the only true God!" This is simply not true! To be sure there are differences in marginal matters, but in the essentials of salvation—and the one true God—all denominations are agreed! The unique core of Christianity, its central message, its heart, is the Gospel—Good News! For nineteen centuries this message has distinguished Christianity! This is its credential! Simply stated it is this: "Christ died for our sins according to the Scriptures; He was buried; He rose again the third day..." (I Corinthians 15:4). It has to do with events primarily, not ideas. It is factual, not theoretical! In this there is no disagreement! All Christian denominations declare Christ to be the road to salvation: "The Way, The Truth, The Life." And they worship the same God, the God and Father of our Lord and Savior Jesus Christ!

The writer went on: "...ministers cannot be inspired when they themselves have to spend so much time proving their point and convincing their flock that only members of their church are the chosen ones." Which is ludicrous! No Christian minister insists his congregation are the chosen ones. In fact the average pastor probably entertains serious doubts in this regard! And the proving he does is rarely polemical. It is instructive, designed to nourish his people and give them a "reason for their hope," a faith that is defensible, realistic, workable.

Fact is there is fundamental unity in the Christian Church. Not unanimity but unity with diversity. The unity of an organism—a body! Christ is the Head! The integrating, consolidating factor is devotion to Him!

"There is one body and one Spirit...one hope...one Lord, one faith, one baptism, one God and Father of all..." (Ephesians 4:4-6).

§ *INESCAPABLE APPOINTMENT*

Some day you are going to answer to God Himself! Nothing in life is surer than this...that every man stands someday before God to give an answer for the "deeds done in the flesh." Daniel Webster once was asked, "What is the greatest thought you have ever had?" Pondering but a moment Webster replied: "The greatest thought I have ever had was of my accountability to God." Without this fact of the ultimate justice of God, the final checks and balance..life is a "tale told by an idiot." Nothing makes sense. Everything is unreasonable.

It is this instinctive knowledge of God's justice in a man's heart that keeps him going. We know that someday there has to be a reckoning. The world is full of injustice of every kind; something has to even it up, level it off. Even those who deny God—or eternity and immortality—cannot deny the idea existing in their heart that something is going to happen someday to punish the wicked and reward the righteous. This is a concept built into the very nature of a man. It is an unshakable conviction—even when we refuse to acknowledge it. The Psalmist said, "I had fainted unless I had believed to see the goodness of God in the land of the living." God Himself has said, "Vengeance is Mine, I will repay!"

But the thing we overlook so often is the realization that if this justice of God is operative, then it includes everyone. It includes me! It includes you! Each of us is directly responsible to God! God is recording in His own way the deeds of men. No only their deeds, but their thoughts, their motives, their private lives. God sees—knows—remembers! Nothing can be hid from Him. There's nowhere a man can go to get away from God; nowhere to hide his actions, to cover his thoughts. Our lives are an open book to Him. He knows us—our secret thoughts, the intent of our hearts.

This is inevitable, unavoidable, inexorable. God is on His Throne! He has not abdicated. He rules behind the scenes in the shadows. God lives! This is the only sensible, reasonable and sane hope in a mad, wild, blundering, idiotic world. You and I will stand before Him someday. We will answer to Him. We are accountable to God. This is one case that can't be "fixed."

"It is appointed unto men once to die, but after that the judgment" (Hebrews 9:27); "In the day when God shall judge the secrets of men by Jesus Christ..." (Romans 2:16).

§ HIS WORD, HIS BOND

"*I*t is the word of a gentleman of the most strict and sacred honor, so that's the end of it!" With this irresistible logic, David Livingstone, the great pioneer missionary to Africa, explained his implicit trust in Jesus Christ. He knew that the word of Jesus could be taken at its face value and upon this word he could rest the whole weight of any problem or need he might encounter in life.

Viewed in this way, the utter simplicity of Christian tranquility is overwhelming. The normal attitude of the Christian should be one of composure and peace. Not in the sense of being oblivious to the realities of life, but Christian normalcy is quietness in the midst of the storm. The storm is real...but so is Jesus Christ. Trusting in the word of Jesus Christ brings calm in the midst of turmoil. Nothing is more humiliating to a man than to have his word doubted. The honorable man prides himself on the fact that "his word is his bond." We often pin our faith to the promise of another and relax in complete confidence that the author of the promise is trustworthy. The job's as good as done because the one to whom it has been entrusted is capable and reliable. Man operates on this basis again and again in day-to-day affairs. How much more ought a man rest in the promise of Jesus Christ!

Here's the secret of Christian composure—Christian triumph. The word of Jesus Christ is the word of a gentleman. It can be taken at face value, trusted implicitly. He is capable and reliable. He cannot fail. Take the worry and anxiety out of life. Examine the promises of Jesus Christ and depend on them. Let His peace reign in your heart.

"My peace I give unto you; not as the world giveth, give I unto you. Let not your heart be troubled..." (John 14:27).

§ ONLY ONE YOU!

"*T*he only Lincoln God hath given to men..."

These words, one line of a poem by Lyman Whitney Allen, stood out on the page as I glanced at a little folder entitled "The Lincoln Pew" while attending New York Avenue Presbyterian Church, Washington,

D.C. Right! There has been only one Lincoln! God never has and never will make another! But that's true of every one of us!

You are the only *you* that God has given to men! When God made you He broke the mold, so to speak. And there'll never be another you! Of course you are important! Every man is! In the economy of God there is no such thing as an unimportant man, no measure for the worth of one individual. "One man is worth more than a whole civilization," wrote one historian. "If only one person responded to the love of God in Christ, it would still have been worthwhile for Him to sacrifice Himself on the cross," said another. "What shall it profit a man if he gain the whole world and lose his soul?" asked Jesus Christ. "What will a man give in exchange for his soul?"

In the infinite variety of His Divine artistry, God makes every man unique and distinctive from all others—as every snowflake is different from all others. And in His matchless plan, God purposes that every man shall have a place in the sun, a job to do, a place to fill. If a man does not fill his place, there is no substitute to step into the breach. Of course life has a way of compensating and getting along even when a man fails to be himself in his place doing his job, but it's not as it could be. Something's lacking! No statistics are able to contain the incalculable loss suffered when one man fails to be himself in the fulfillment of God's plan for him. Like the ripples stirred by a pebble dropped in a brook, a man's influence moves out from him to concentric circles affecting for good or ill every life over which it flows.

A father fails and his whole family suffers. The son is something less than he should be because the father did not live up to himself. And every life the son touches is secondarily affected by the father's influence on the son. Of course you are important! Fail to be the God-filled, God-ruled, God-led man you were intended to be, and you leave a great big hole in life! Family, colleagues, friends suffer a loss because you failed to fulfill yourself. Only God can make a man himself. Only God can make a man all he was intended to become. Let God run your life. He frees you to be yourself!

"I say...to every man...not to think of himself more highly than he ought to think; but to think soberly as God hath dealt to every man the measure of faith" (Romans 12:3).

§ *CONFIDENCE THAT IS NOT MISLEADING*

*F*avorable circumstances do not necessarily indicate Divine favor any more than adversity is an evidence of God's disfavor. This is one of the subtle satanic traps that mislead the Christian...the implication that when circumstances are favorable all is well or when they are unfavorable God is displeased.

It is not uncommon for a man to rationalize his sin simply because the roof does not fall in on him. He thinks he's getting away with it because judgment does not fall immediately. As a matter of fact, he thinks, "Things have never been better. God must not be displeased with what I am doing." But one of the stubborn facts of life is the prosperity of the wicked... And the suffering of the righteous! Rains fall and the sun shines on the unjust as well as the just.

Furthermore the Prince of this world has the power to bless those who serve him! He is quite willing to surround with favorable circumstances those who are willing to cooperate with his program. His Satanic Majesty wasn't "born yesterday!" He knows his way around. He's a master at making sin look reasonable—and profitable!

Remember also that God does not settle His accounts in a day. The final settlement is the important one! Just because life smiles on a man is not necessarily dependable criteria that he is in the will of God. And the fact that life roughs up a man doesn't always mean he is out of God's will. Never forget that the only perfect Man who ever lived suffered more than any other man in history, according to the will of God.

Let a man examine his motives, not his circumstances. Let him be sure that the most important thing is the will of God for him. Let his ambitions and desires and aspirations be subservient to the will of God. Then whatever circumstances may be he will be guided by an enlightened conscience. He may know he must proceed against unfavorable circumstances...or he may be restrained from proceeding in spite of favorable circumstances. God's guidance is inward. The test is whether or not a man consciously makes every other thing subserve God's will.

"Beloved, if our heart condemn us not, then have we confidence toward God" (I John 3:21); "Commit thy way unto the Lord; trust also in Him; and He shall bring it to pass" (Psalm 37:5).

§ *DIRECTION*

*R*adar-equipped!
Stands for the ultimate in air-travel safety! It guarantees the smoothest possible flight—gives maximum assurance of arrival at destination. Regardless of the weather!

Radar doesn't eliminate bad flying conditions, but it enables a man to fly without being victimized by them. The weather's there, but a man can fly above, or around it, and land safely at his destination as though flying conditions were perfect. Of course a man may ignore radar as though it doesn't exist. He can get fussy, concerned and fearful over the weather and refuse to fly—and deprive himself of the comfort and security radar is designed to give. How much better to reckon on this fantastic device, relax and enjoy the trip.

Tomorrow is going to have its share of tempests and storms. That man is unrealistic who ignores them or heeds any simple panacea which promises to eliminate them. But wise the man who chooses to be God-directed. That is the ultimate in wisdom!

God does not promise immunity from trouble; but He does promise to make that man who obeys Him "more than a conqueror." God does not guarantee the weather, but He does guarantee to take a man through it! In fact, the man who is led by God will discover that God actually is able to turn trouble and tragedy into triumph. God uses difficulty to make the man...makes difficulty serve the man. (You'll not escape the bunkers and sand traps in the future, but under God's direction, they will be made to improve your game.)

It's your decision! You can choose to fly blind...or you can choose now and daily to allow God to guide you. You may choose to disregard God...or to obey Him. He waits only for your consent, your submission, your surrender.

"Commit thy way unto the Lord, trust also in Him, and He shall bring it to pass" (Psalm 37:5); "We know that all things work together for good to them that love God; to them that are called according to His purpose" (Romans 8:28).

§ *INTELLIGENT SUBMISSION*

*S*urrender can mean either defeat...or victory!

There is the surrender of a defeated foe to his conqueror; and the submission of a subordinate to his chief! One is involuntary and humiliating—the surrender of the broken sword. The other is intelligent submission to authority—wise recognition of a systematic order and voluntary conformity to that order.

It is the man who has learned to obey his superiors that inspires obedience in others. He who will not recognize authority and yield to it, repudiates his right to the place of authority. Having no respect for properly constituted management, he will never win respect as a manager. The good follower gains the following!

That is the heart of leadership! The best leader is the best follower! He commands men's allegiance because he knows how to knuckle under to command.

This is preeminently true in the realm of the spirit. Some men never learn submission and obedience to God until circumstances bring them to their knees in humiliation. In false pride a man refuses to admit his dependence upon God and his rightful conformity to God's will... until broken by adversity and tragedy, he surrenders and lays down his arms like an enemy capitulating.

Sad that God must break a man before He can make a man of him! Stupid, senseless, stubborn pride (the root of secularism) always robs a man of God's best. Knowledgeable is the man who bows to the Lordship of Christ, who gladly yields to His loving mastery and enjoys the inexpressible pleasure of His Godly reign in life. Self-defeated the man who for whatever reason will not submit to Christ!

"Why call ye Me Lord, Lord, and do not the things which I say?" (Luke 6:46).

§ *CURE FOR INFERIORITY COMPLEX*

*E*ver felt like a grasshopper—unimportant, inferior, low down? The twelve princes of Israel did when Moses sent them to spy out the Promised Land: "And there we saw the giants...and we were in our own sight as grasshoppers..." (Numbers 13:33). They were impressed with the land, a land flowing with milk and honey, a land of unbelievable fertility, a land of incalculable promise... But they were also impressed with the inhabitants of the land. So impressed, in fact, that they were whipped before they started. The princes of Israel were overwhelmed with inferiority. It was inevitable that they project this inferiority upon the inhabitants: "...we were in our own sight as grasshoppers, and so we were in their sight." This was not true as subsequent events revealed, but this is the double deception of the inferiority complex: One not only feels that he is inferior, but he thinks everybody else feels that way about him.

Joshua's spies found the facts to be absolutely the contrary. They were told by a native, "Your terror is fallen upon us and all the inhabitants faint because of you...our hearts did melt, neither did there remain any more courage in any man, because of you" (Joshua 2:9, 11). Contrast the defeatism of the spies in Numbers 13:31 with the invincibility of the spies of Joshua 2:24, "Truly the Lord hath delivered into our hands all the land..." Moses' spies absolutely convinced of defeat. Joshua's spies absolutely certain of victory. How do you account for the radical difference? The princes of Israel trusted in themselves! Joshua's spies trusted in God! The first measured their chances of victory by their own human resources; the second reckoned on the infinite resources of Almighty God.

The man who trusts in himself sooner or later feels like a grasshopper in his own sight...and he thinks everybody else feels the same about him. As long as circumstances are all right, he makes out; but when life tumbles in, he crawls. The only confidence he has is self-confidence—and in the pinches that's sheer delusion! What a difference in the man who has God-confidence! He's invincible because he counts on the resources of God, not on his own weak, limited assets. He is certain of victory because he is absolutely sure of the Victor!

"I can do all things through Christ who strengthens me!" (Philippians 4:13).

§ *NOTHING IS SECULAR FOR THE CHRISTIAN*

Secular or sacred—what's the distinction? Is this a legitimate dichotomy for the Christian? Does he live in two contrasting or conflicting departments: going to church, singing in the choir, or serving as a church officer is sacred; whereas his job, his recreation, his social life is secular? Is a Christian supposed to keep "changing hats"?

Little is known of Jesus between twelve and thirty: At twelve He confounded the teachers in the Temple with His depth and insight. After this we read, "And He went down with them [His parents] and came to Nazareth, and was obedient to them" (Luke 2:51). Time and again Jesus was recognized as "the carpenter's son," or "the carpenter" which indicates that much of His life was spent in a carpenter's shop: first as an apprentice to His father; later as a master craftsman. Thirty of His thirty-three years were spent in obscurity in a small village, plying a trade like the rest of His neighbors half those years. He mastered the use of hammer, chisel and saw...and it does not take a too active imagination to picture the beauty and perfection of His work.

But the point is, were those fifteen years (more or less) at a carpenter's bench secular? Was the great bulk of Jesus' life secular? Was less than one tenth of His life dedicated to sacred pursuits? The answer is obvious! Everything Jesus did was sacred! Giving sight to the blind, healing the sick, raising the dead, cleansing the leper, restoring a fallen woman, teaching on a hillside, or making a cabinet. Everything Jesus touched was sacred! Because life came from the Father, belonged to the Father. Everything Jesus thought or said or did was for the Father's sake!

And so it is for the Christian. Work is as sacred as worship! What a man does in his office Monday morning is as sacred as what he did in church the day before. What he does any night in the week is as sacred as his meeting with the deacons or with the choir. If what a man does during the week is not sacred, neither is what he does on Sunday in the sanctuary. Christianity is an around-the-clock proposition—seven days a week! Everything is sacred...or nothing is!

"Whether therefore you eat or drink, whatsoever therefore you do, do all to the glory of God" (I Corinthians 10:31).

§ *THE PRICE OF PROGRESS*

*T*hank God for detours! They spell progress.

People fuss (so do I) when they have to go around instead of through...but watch those same people when the job's done. They go sailing along, deeply contented with the broad, smooth, uninterrupted concrete ribbon. The detours are forgotten in the thrill of the new expressway.

The wise man takes difficulty as part of the process, never as final. Foolish man wants to have his cake and eat it too. He wants the turnpike, without the detour. But you don't get one without the other. That's life! New home going up in the neighborhood...everything's a mess: bricks, stone, mortar, wood, scaffolding, dirt. Pavement's dusty; yard's cluttered; trucks coming and going—pounding, sawing, clattering... Then the new house is finished; the rubble cleared away; lawn seeded. And the whole neighborhood benefits.

It's the immature man, the adolescent, who wants progress without the price. He looks for the "royal road" to knowledge without the blood, sweat and tears of study. He's got his eyes on the "easy buck." He's everlastingly waiting for a break, the quick, easy payoff. Like the guy at the slot machine, pouring in nickels, hoping for the jackpot. He doesn't seem to understand that life is good business, not a gamble. Its dividends are the interest on investment, not the chancy flood of nickels occasionally vomited out by a fixed one-armed bandit.

Real tragedy of the slot-machine philosophy is that inevitably you put in more than you get out. You can't cheat life! Try to make it the easy way. You never make it...and the price is exorbitant!

"He which soweth sparingly shall reap also sparingly; and he which soweth bountifully shall reap also bountifully" (II Corinthians 9:6).

§ THE SANCTITY OF SUFFERING

*T*he tragedy is not that a man suffers, but that he suffers for nothing, or for an unworthy cause. Suffering is inescapable, an ingredient of life, a stubborn fact. Suffering cannot be avoided by pretending it is not. Evasion is weakness, not wisdom. Ignoring the reality does not eliminate the problem.

The choice is not whether a man will suffer, but what he suffers for! Some men suffer to make a success in business or a career. Some suffer to make a million dollars. Others suffer to become famous, or popular, or powerful; to gain position or influence or prestige. Suffering is the "stuff" of human greatness; the raw material of character when taken rightly. It gives dimension to life: depth, understanding, strength, soundness.

It sweeps the shallowness out of life.

Of course a man may grow bitter through suffering; but this only compounds the tragedy, makes suffering doubly disastrous; lets it hurt twice: when it happens and after it is over. Embittered by suffering, a man turns hard and brittle. And usually the man embittered by suffering is the one who suffers for a worthless cause, or no cause at all. Suffering is meaningless, purposeless, because he has no standards, no principles, nor worthy goals; nothing to die for, or live for!

The man who lives for a cause worthy enough to die for makes suffering serve him, serve his high purpose. And suffering becomes a bonafide asset.

"It is better to fail in a cause that will ultimately succeed than to succeed in a cause that will ultimately fail" (Peter Marshall).

"Endure hardness as a good soldier of Jesus Christ" (II Timothy 2:3).

§ BEGINNING OF WISDOM

*W*hat do you think of God?"

G. K. Chesterton used to say that if he were seeking a lodging he would ask his landlady that question. Knowing her answer to that, he would know her attitude in most other important things. It is not so far-fetched either. How a man feels about God predetermines pretty much how he will feel and think about everything worthwhile. A man's attitude toward God is basic. Believe wrong about God and that wrong idea or attitude will distort everything else about your life. Like believing for example that 2 plus 2 equals 5. How would you conduct business on that basis? Nor can a man live rationally and consistently with reality if he holds the wrong attitude toward life's basic reality which is God. Begin wrongly with God, a man pays the price of such an idea sooner or later. He cannot escape the consequences of wrong thinking about God.

Men have juggled figures over a long period to hide dishonest manipulating of funds, but it does not last. Sooner or later the laws of accounting intervene and show up the discrepancy. This is precisely the reason some intellectuals, so-called, do not see anything wrong in Communism; their rejection of God causes them to be blind to the basic and diabolical opposition of Communism to our way of life.

The plain fact is the real trouble in the world today can be directly traced to improper diagnosis. We have assumed that man's dilemma is due entirely to the man-to-man relationship and ignored the God-man relationship. Evidence of this lies in what men think of Jesus Christ. This is the clearest picture of man's desire to leave God out of the picture. The Bible is quite explicit in this: that to reject Christ is to reject God. Jesus said to the Pharisees, "If God were your Father, you would believe Me, for I came from God, and I go to God." And this rejection of Christ infects the whole of modern life, individually and collectively.

It is like living upside down, all values, all realities are inverted. Man is a caricature; life is irrational. It is your business if you wish to ignore God, but then do not complain when your life does not enjoy the benefits of a God-ordered world.

"The fear of the Lord is the beginning of wisdom..." (Psalm 111:10).

§ SATIATED AND STARVED

*P*ity the man who starves his imagination; who rarely ever gives his soul a chance to stretch and breathe. Busy on the job all day, buried in a dimly lit bar after work, nose in the paper on the way home; dinner over, TV until bedtime. Busy, busy, busy, nose to the grindstone, shoulder to the wheel; financial page between cocktails and dinner, then the tyrant of TV. What a diet for the soul!

Even on the golf course, surrounded with God's expansive beauty, he is victimized by a little white pill he beats to death to break 90; then the 19th hole and a bar again. And if he mentions God, it is only when he slices into the rough or misses a putt.

How long since you fed your soul on a sunrise or a sunset or really feasted on the sheer luxury of blue sky and fleecy clouds? Have you noticed lately the vaulted heaven on a black night, stars like gold dust everywhere?

When was the last time you thought about God, His love and providence; the benefits with which He has endowed you, the Divine care your family has enjoyed? How often do you thank God for good food or clean sheets, for a faithful wife and precious children, for friendships and a good job, for health and strength, a whole body, for sight and hearing and speech?

What are you feeding your mind? Pulp magazines, cheap entertainment, smut; do you force your mind to exist on garbage? Or do you nourish it with deep thought, with dimension and depth? Do you ever allow it to feast on God's Word? Do you ever challenge your mind? You spend hundreds of dollars on things that are about as nourishing as sawdust; and the Bread from Heaven is a gift of God!

God offers you absolutely free air and water, trees and flowers, mountains and valleys, streams and lakes, sun and moon and stars. How desperately hungry your soul is for that which costs you nothing! With abounding wealth God surrounds you, and you submit your soul to a pale, thin, watered-down diet of crumbs and stale left-overs for which you pay a small fortune. What irony: God gives us an incalculable legacy in Jesus Christ, and we pauperize our souls!

"My soul thirsteth for God, for the living God..." (Psalm 42:2).

"My soul longeth, yea, even fainteth for the courts of the Lord: my heart and my flesh crieth out for the living God" (Psalm 84:2).

§ *CLEANLINESS IS NEXT TO GODLINESS*

*W*hy shower every morning?

Because your body craves cleanliness. Dirt is for gardens, not bodies, and a man is happiest when clean. Uncleanness destroys confidence and poise, a fact which pays off for Madison Avenue in selling soap and toothpaste.

Of course a man can adjust to dirt, get to the place where it doesn't make any difference. Some men on skid row haven't had a bath in months; they stink, but the smell doesn't bother them. They couldn't care less about filth, which is the awful price a man pays for neglecting bodily cleanliness.

The same is true of a man's soul! Made to be Godly, it craves purity, longs for spiritual health; but it can get used to dirt! Neglect your soul and it will settle down in a rut, adapt itself to the gutter if you keep it there long enough. No matter how repugnant it is to others, you won't be aware of it. Sin's master tactic is to make its victim insensitive to its operation. Force your soul to live with smut, it will adjust eventually and quit wanting holiness!

Neglect your soul beyond the point where it no longer cares, where it loses its aspiration for the clean, pure, robust righteousness for which it was made; there is no limit to the level of savagery, brutality, filth and shame to which you can sink. Like a "dog returning to its vomit" or "the pig to wallowing in its mire," a man can get so accustomed to spiritual squalor that he is unhappy anywhere else!

"...when they knew God, they glorified Him not as God, neither were thankful; but became vain in their imaginations, and their foolish heart was darkened. Professing themselves to be wise they became fools, and changed the glory of the uncorruptible God into an image made like to corruptible man, and to birds and fourfooted beasts, and creeping things. Wherefore God gave them up to uncleanness through the lusts of their own hearts..." (Romans 1:21-24).

"Blessed are those who hunger and thirst for righteousness, for they shall be satisfied" (Matthew 5:6).

§ *THE WORST HUNGER IS GOD HUNGER*

*Y*ou reach the point of diminishing returns so quickly.

It does not take long for a luxury to become a necessity; then new luxuries are desired which in turn are soon taken for granted as necessities, and so on ad nauseam. Life becomes saturated without contentment; indeed discontent seems to flourish as acquisitions increase.

Satiated but not satisfied, the dreadful lot of many pathetic Americans who seem to have everything but it adds up to zero! One car to a family used to be a luxury, now two are a necessity. Life seemed to go along when men traveled by train, now the jets are becoming too slow; like the man in a cartoon who arrived at his New York office, threw his briefcase down in disgust and snapped at his secretary, "Might as well have walked, it took me seven hours to fly from Los Angeles." Some men cannot even stand to miss one section of a revolving door!

The average man figures he would relax and take it easy if he had a quarter million dollars put away; but when he gets it, he finds he cannot stop and goes for half a million. When money is security, never is there enough! Our appetites are insatiable. No matter what we have we want more, and the more we get the less we appreciate what we have, the more discontented we are until we have something else.

Of course, because in the final analysis man was made for God and only God can really satisfy him. God hunger is the worst kind of hunger, and until this basic need is met, nothing else man has or does can satisfy!

This is the clue to human restlessness, to discontent, to interminable dissatisfaction in life. This is the root of anxiety!

"Thou hast made us for Thyself, O God, and restless are our hearts 'til they find their rest in Thee" (St. Augustine).

"Delight thyself also in the Lord, and He shall give thee the desires of thine heart" (Psalm 37:4).

PAUPERS IN THE MIDST OF PLENTY

*W*hat a pity to live like a pauper when one has a million dollars in the bank!

Unbelievable, yet this is precisely the condition of many men. They have not begun to avail themselves of the resources which God in His love has provided for them. They are begging bread, spiritually speaking, not realizing that the Son of God has made a priceless deposit in their favor upon which they can draw at any time and in any amount whatever the need. The hitch comes at the point where a man either refuses to recognize his need or is too proud to admit it.

Of course it is not quite that simple. Pride is not that obvious usually. Pride is extraordinarily subtle and deceptive. Pride would probably put it like this: "I don't deserve God's help and blessing, therefore I cannot expect it." What man does deserve God's blessing? Certainly the man who thinks he does is of all men least worthy. That is consummate pride. No man merits God's favor!

That is the whole point of the love of God: It is expressed in grace, and *grace* means *undeserved favor*! God does not draw a line and say to man, "You come up to this line and I will bless you." On the contrary, God goes way over the line to meet man wherever he has a need. This is the significance of grace. Grace is God's love lavished on man!

Reason God cannot bless a man is not that he is unworthy, it is that the man will not receive the blessing. This is the supreme expression of man's declaration of independence from God. This is the subtle, insidious, quiet rebellion of secular man! And by a clever twist of reason man repudiates God's gifts on the ground that he does not deserve them. This is really man's way of saying, "I don't need God!"

The religion of the bible (Old and New Testaments) was designed for sinners, and men who refuse to acknowledge their sin usually have no use for the Bible. For it declares quite bluntly that *all men* are sinners: "All have sinned and come short of the glory of God. There is none righteous, not one!" Proud men repudiate the Bible and God's gifts with this perversion of good sense: feeling they are really not sinners, they refuse to receive God's gifts by pretending that they feel they are unworthy. Of course there are men who honestly feel unworthy of

God's blessing. Such men must realize that this attitude, if honest before God, is the very thing that qualifies a man for God's grace. Need is the one prerequisite. When a man admits his need, and seeks God's help, he gets it! It is as simple as that!

"Blessed are they that hunger and thirst after righteousness for they shall be filled" (Matthew 5:6). All a man needs is the will—the desire; God has the supply. Wherever a man has the appetite, God will do the filling!

§ LIFE WITH A CAPITAL "L"

*A*re you starving your soul?

You eat three square meals a day, and try to get proper rest and exercise for the sake of your body. Do you leave your soul undernourished, weak, anemic? Bodily health is important, but soul health is infinitely more so! ("What shall it profit a man if he gains the whole world, and loses his soul?")

Modern man is so easily absorbed in the physical, so prone to be indifferent to the spiritual; he is apt to major in the temporal, ignore the eternal. Here is the key to much of modern exhaustion and frustration. Man battles to keep the body in shape, lets his soul go to pot, and wonders why he is petering out! He feels drained all the time. Wakes up in the morning less rested than when he went to bed. He goes to work because he must, not because he wants to.

Life loses its vitality and drive. It is pale, thin, uninteresting, unchallenging. Living is drudgery, a duty instead of a privilege. So he goes on the pill and tonic routine, resorts to cocktails for pick-up. But the help is only temporary; he begins to get satisfaction in inverse ratio to the amount of pills and tonic and cocktails. Their power to pick up diminishes fast! Finally the cure becomes as dull and boring and monotonous as the disease.

The man is fed up!

His body is saturated with attention; his soul is dried up with neglect. He has put everything on that which is destined to rot in a grave; abandoned that which was meant to live forever!

What kind of a fool is man anyway?

And to compound the problem, he justifies his neglect by letting himself be talked out of faith. He argues himself out of belief in Christ and eternity; but deep inside him his soul cries out for recognition, languishes for attention. Get wise, man! You were made for fellowship with God. Life begins with Christ!

"This is life eternal, that they might know Thee, the only true God, and Jesus Christ whom Thou hast sent" (John 17:3).

§ *LIFE WORKS BY ITSELF*

*E*ver hear a man say, "Health is okay, but you've got to apply it"? Of course not! Health applies itself. If a man is healthy, the application will follow through.

Normally the application of health or strength is automatic. A man does that which contributes to his health (food, rest, exercise, etc.) and other things being equal, the health and strength will assert themselves in every area of life: home, office, shop and club. A man does not worry about how he is going to apply it, he just keeps healthy. His health makes a difference in everything he does. In fact, the man who is strong and healthy cannot conceal it. It is obvious, benefits his whole life.

Christianity works this way too. Real Christianity! You keep hearing men say, "It's okay, but you've got to apply it." That is entirely the wrong slant. The fellow that talks that way got his idea somewhere besides the Bible. He thinks Christianity is a set of rules a man endorses, then struggles to live up to. If he fails to live up to the rules, he is not applying his Christianity. So goes this kind of reasoning. Just man doing his best! That is not Biblical. It is actually in opposition to the Bible.

Christianity is life—life that is a gift of God through Jesus Christ, God's Son. It is not something a man does; it is something a man receives when he begins to take Christ seriously. It is not man making his best effort; it is much more than that. It is God doing something to a man, in a man, through a man. Christianity is putting one's trust in Jesus Christ, feeding on the Word of God by regular use of the Bible; joining in fellowship and worship with other Christians; prayer. These are the means whereby the Christian man grows strong spiritually.

Having met the conditions for spiritual health, its application is automatic in his life. Everything he does is benefited by spiritual strength. It gives tone, sharpness, balance and efficiency. One man struggling to live like a Christian, fails! Another man, knowing the secret, follows the simple conditions for spiritual health. Being a Christian is natural, effortless and real.

"Blessed is the man...that delighteth in the law of the Lord and in His law doth he meditate day and night. He shall be like a tree planted by rivers of living water that bringeth forth his fruit in season..." (Psalm 1:1-3).

§ THE POWER OF THE GOSPEL

Trouble is we try too hard, get all tied up in knots! We have the idea Christianity is a matter of trial and error, a struggle to be good, which becomes for many an almost futile effort to live up to some impossible rigid moral or religious rules. It leaves a man guilty of the pride of achievement (which is self-righteousness), or guilty of the despair of failure (which is to discount God's grace). Or what is perhaps worse, he levels out on the horrible, dull, deadening plateau of mediocrity and neutralism, just going mechanically through the motions of being a Christian without much hope of succeeding, yet dogged by the terrible fear of failure.

Plenty of men grow weary of this and finally throw in the sponge, give up the whole deal as a bad job. Getting fed up with religion they drop it altogether. Or others settle for an easy satisfaction and delude themselves into believing that just "doing the best one can" is all that Christianity amounts to anyway. Their religion takes on a kind of averageness which is a reproach to the name of Christian. This neither satisfies the man who follows it nor does it interest others. In fact, it alienates them. Seeing this colorless, anemic caricature of Christianity they say, "If that's Christianity, I want none of it."

What a far cry this is from the living, breathing, throbbing, driving dynamic of the Christianity we read about in the New Testament. The heart of their faith was not a struggle; not that they were perfect, or any less human that we. It was simply that their normal, average, mundane, regular lives had been capitvated and invaded by a Superhuman Person!

Christianity to them was not a difficult, and often seemingly hopeless, struggle to be good. Those first-century Christians would never have laid down their lives in the arena (as thousands did) just for the sake of struggling to be good. To them it meant a new loyalty, a new affection, a new surrender of themselves to the most fascinating Person who ever lived. They were men possessed by Jesus Christ! As far as they were concerned God Himself had come to earth. With glorious abandon they gave themselves to Him and declared everywhere the tremendous fact that "God was in Christ reconciling the world to Himself."

Their power was their message! Their message was "Christ crucified and risen again." This they heralded to all who would listen. This was the "power of God unto salvation." This is it! Not man's best effort alone, or with God's help. Not man doing the best he can, but the Good News that God has done for man what he cannot do for himself.

"God so loved the world, that He gave His only begotten Son, that whosoever believeth in Him should not perish, but have everlasting life" (John 3:16).

§ BELIEF IS WITH THE HEART, NOT THE HEAD

*B*elief, in the final analysis, is a matter of will.

A man chooses what he is going to believe or disbelieve.

Take for example the case of an eminently successful business executive who in a recent conversation utterly ridiculed the idea of everlasting life. His attitude was that belief in life after death could not possibly be held by an intelligent person. To him immortality was an invention of preachers to scare people. As we discussed this belief it was obvious that he had no evidence to support his position; he had no ground for believing that there is no life beyond the grave, but he believed it vehemently. It was pointed out that belief in immortality is as old as man; that it is a universal belief, that the man who disbelieves in it is the exception rather than the rule; that Jesus Christ taught it; that in fact the weight of the evidence was wholly on the side of a belief in life after death; but he simply ignored the evidence, clung to his belief more tenaciously than ever.

This is typical of many who are indifferent to Jesus Christ. They say they cannot believe without proof, yet their unbelief is unsupported by proof.

A man rejects Christ, not through lack of evidence (his disbelief is not based on evidence) but simply because he refuses to believe regardless of the evidence. Actually no way of life is more defensible than the Christian way! No view of life is as realistic, as consistent with things as they are, as is the Christian view. The man who rejects Jesus Christ as Savior and Lord does so in the face of incontrovertible proof; and incidentally he demonstrates the irrational nature of unbelief.

It is not difficult to find an excuse for not believing in Jesus Christ, but there are no intelligent reasons for rejection. Do not deprive yourself of God's gracious gift to the peril of your eternal soul.

"He who believes in the Son has eternal life; he who does not obey the Son shall not see life, but the wrath of God rests upon him" (John 3:36 [RSV]).

§ *FACTS AND THE FACT!*

*F*aith does not disregard facts!
On the contrary, it is the essence of faith that it rests upon facts! Faith without facts is meaningless, wishful thinking or self-delusion. The question is, what facts does a man count on for faith? What facts take precedence in his calculations? Does a man give precedence to primary facts, or secondary ones; to eternal facts, or temporary ones?

Clouds are a fact, but they do not eliminate the fact of the sun! An overcast does not mean the sun has stopped shining! The overcast is a fact, but so is the sun! And the sun will be there long after the overcast is dispelled. Trouble is too many men believe in the overcast instead of the sun! They let themselves get preoccupied with secondary facts and get all fussy and bothered. How ridiculous to allow clouds to destroy one's faith in the sun!

Yet day after day men allow the clouds of circumstances to rob them of faith in the Son of God!

Of course the circumstances are fact, but so is the Son of God! He is One Supreme Fact upon which a man can count whatever the circumstances may be. These are the facts upon which the faith of the Christian rests: The entrance into history of the One Perfect Man; the perfection of His life; the sacrificial nature of His death; His bodily Resurrection from the dead; the bonafide promise of His return!

God has acted in history, and the fact of God's action in history, in His Son, is the "stuff" which makes Christian faith valid and relevant. God continues to act in history. Jesus Christ is contemporary. No Christian need be overcome by the facts of difficult or tragic circumstances, for greater far is the supreme fact of God's love in Christ. Difficult circumstances only prove the validity of faith. Like muscle, faith grows with exercise. Exercise involves resistance and it is the resistance of reverses that develops strong faith.

You decide which facts you are going to believe, the facts of difficult days, or the fact of God's love and providence!

"Commit thy way unto the Lord; trust also in Him; and He shall bring it to pass" (Psalm 37:5).

§ AUTHENTIC CHRISTIANITY

*C*ore of Christianity is not a proposition, but a Person.

Heart of the Christian message is not an ideology, but a Man, the God-Man.

Ground of Christian faith is neither ethics nor theology, but the Savior.

A man will never understand the faith that has made Western civilization possible and the greatness of America a reality until he understands this: that the center of Christian faith and allegiance is a Person, the most fascinating Person who ever lived, a Man utterly unique from all other men. His character was unimpeachable, His teaching the highest and finest human minds ever contemplated. He was a perfect Man in thought, word and deed. His earthly ministry ended on a cross, but that cross was not an interruption, it was the *goal* of His earthly life. He had come to die. He had come to lay down His life on the cross!

Christianity involves much more than the mere acceptance of theological propositions or ethical precepts or ideological speculations. It goes infinitely deeper than a man's effort simply to apply Christian principles. (To hold that the Christian solution is a matter merely of man's correct application of the teachings of Jesus is to be pitifully naive about Jesus, His teaching, human nature itself, the lessons of history and the status quo.)

Christianity is infinitely more than human effort; it is God at work in and through man as man consents to the Divine activity. Christianity consists basically in the acceptance of and commitment to a Person, the Lord Jesus Christ. A man is a Christian, not simply because he embraces Christian teaching or ethics and ideas and strives to live up to them; he is a Christian who receives a Person, puts his trust in that Person, builds his life around obedience to that Person.

Christian faith is not primarily propositional, it is primarily personal. It is the personal relationship between a man and Jesus Christ. The Bible teaches that "all things were made by Christ and for Christ!" He is the King whose Kingdom is eternal. In its essence Christian faith is total allegiance to the King of kings! As men commit themselves to the King, His Kingdom increases on this earth. As men obey the King, the blessings of His Kingdom are extended on this earth.

But that is not all; the final fruit of Christ's reign in the heart of man will be that day when "the kingdoms of this world shall become the kingdoms of our Lord and of His Christ."

§ *THE ULTIMATE ANSWER*

*I*f men would only follow the Golden Rule.
   If they would only live up to the Sermon on the Mount.
   If they would only practice brotherhood.
   So much wringing of hands and "if"ing.
   If only men would not get cancer. If only they would not contract

disease. Imagine the medical profession wringing its hands, just wishing somehow that men would stop getting sick. Or imagine a physician scolding a patient for his illness, then dismissing him without recommending a cure. Grateful we are that medical science does more than scold and admonish and rebuke and pontificate. Medical science will not rest until it finds a cure for disease.

Fact is men do not follow the Golden Rule; men do not live up to the Sermon on the Mount; men do not act like brothers. But scolding and pontificating is not the answer. Wishing they would change does not help, nor does "if"ing.

Man's failure to square with the Golden Rule or the Sermon on the Mount or brotherhood is not the problem, it is the symptom. The problem is an inborn enmity toward God, and irrational, malignant antipathy in the human heart. It is a spiritual disease.

And there is a cure!

It is the Gospel of Jesus Christ, "the power of God unto salvation to everyone that believeth, to the Jew first and also to the Greek." We need not the wringing of hands, not the viewing with alarm; we need the preaching of the Gospel, the faithful witness of Christians to its relevancy in their lives.

Jesus said, "That which cometh out of the man, that defileth the man. For from within out of the heart of men, proceed evil thoughts..." (Mark 7:20, 21).

§ TRUE HOLINESS

Holiness and ethics are not identical.

A truly holy man will be ethical, but the ethical man is not necessarily holy. One may be totally irreligious and at the same time quite ethical. Atheists (so-called) often lead highly respectable lives; many eminent men of history have been out and out *un*believers. Church people do not have a corner on ethics and morals in America; plenty non-church-goers lead good lives. (Be it remembered, however, that they are the product of a Judeo-Christian culture; they received their ethical norm and momentum from a civilization born out of a Biblical heritage.)

Authentic holiness is infinitely more than ethics and morals. Holiness has to do with man's inner condition. What health is to the body, holiness is to the soul. It is to be "whole," to be spiritually fit. It is to be rightly oriented with God, to be God-centered; it is to belong to the Lord, to be His servant, His friend.

Holiness has to do with life's purpose and meaning. The truly holy man lives for the glory of God. Whatever he does, whatever his vocation, his profession, his "call," he is in it for God's glory. This is the real glory of man. Glory of a thing is its purpose: glory of the rose is beauty and fragrance; glory of the bird is its plummage and song; glory of the animal is to serve man (dog is man's best friend).

And the glory of man is to glorify God!

Good works which exalt man, bring commendation only to him, are something less than holiness. Jesus said, "Let your light so shine before men, that they may see your good works, and glorify your Father in Heaven" (Matthew 5:16). True holiness is unselfconscious. The holy man does not think he is holy, the man who thinks he is holy is not! Holiness is not self-generated; it is not of man's doing, it is the gift of God. It is literally the light of Christ shining in and through man.

"They who are righteous live by faith..." (Romans 1:17 [paraphrase]).

§ *TOO PROUD TO RECEIVE*

*S*ometimes the hardest thing a man does is accept a gift! Conditioned from childhood to be self-reliant, he gets the idea that anything he does not pay for is charity, and charity is a disgrace. Strongly indoctrinated with what William D. Whyte, Jr. (The Organization Man) calls, "the protestant ethic," he goes for "rugged individualism" with a strong dose of the "there's-plenty-of-room-at-the-top" philosophy. Being a self-made man is the mark of success, so the hard-headed businessman is inclined to treat with contempt anything that comes easy or has no price tag attached.

Paying his own way is almost an obsession, and he prides himself on the fact that he's had to "go it alone," and what he has was "hard to come by." He enjoys a rather smug satisfaction in the blood, sweat and tears of attainment. Which is right as far as it goes, but it can be carried too far. Satisfaction in accomplishment may be replaced by conceit. Pride can destroy the fruit of achievement, and deprive a man of some of life's greatest gifts.

There is no price tag on the beauties of nature: the mystery of desert vastness, the majesty of the mountain, a stream filled with glittering trout, the glory of sunrise and sunset, the rainbow and the cloud; the unaccountable, indescribable, sheer luxury God has lavished upon the world. They are as free as the air for any man who takes them. But a man may have his nose so close to the grindstone that he loses the capacity to enjoy God's extravagant blessings. Chained to a desk, he becomes a slave to his achievement.

Even love (which, incidentally, cannot be bought) becomes meaningless.

Worst of all, such a philosophy may deprive a man of the supreme gift of God which is eternal life through His Son. Eternal life is a gift; it cannot be purchased, nor will it ever be deserved. It is free, but it is not cheap! It cost God the priceless gift of His Son on the cross, the costliest gift ever offered. Pity the hard-headed businessman who has let drive and self-reliance go to his head and closes the door of his heart upon the greatest asset of all, eternal life through Jesus Christ.

"For God so loved the world, that He gave His only begotten Son, that whosoever believeth in Him should not perish, but have everlasting life" (John 3:16); "To as many as received Christ, to them He gave the power to become the sons of God..." (John 1:12).

§ *WHO'S TO BLAME?*

*G*et right down to it, nobody's to blame for anything!

We figure the Germans started World War II; they blame Hitler, who blamed the Old Order and the Treaty of Versailles, etc. The "Japs" made an unprovoked attack on Pearl Harbor; they blame America's humiliation of the Japanese; America blames California for that discrimination. Who's to blame for Hiroshima and Nagasaki? The men in the B-25's? Pilot or bombardier? Einstein? His equation started it all! Scientists in general? Or Roosevelt? He ordered the exorbitant appropriation for research; but the University of California had the first cyclotron. Let's blame Khrushchev; but Peking is pushing him! Take the race question. Obviously the South's to blame; it's the Supreme Court; or the Chief Justice.

Inflation? That's Labor with its insatiable demand for raises and fringe benefits. No, it's Management and its greed for profit. Actually, it's Wall Street and the bankers. Or Johnson and the Democrats? Or Eisenhower and the Republicans? Is Congress to blame? Maybe back of it all is Marx or Lenin!

It's Hoffa or Beck, Capitalism or Socialism, Communism or Fascism, Protestants or Jews or Roman Catholics, preachers or layment or the Church, Cuba or Castro, or the CIA or the State Deppartment; it's Hollywood or the newspapers, writers or editors, but "Whoever's to blame, it's not I! I'm clean; don't look at me!" We go through life inventing scapegoats, and when we get through passing the buck, nobody's to blame for anything! Except perhaps God, or the devil. We all have an alcoholic nature; but all of us do not find our escape in the bottle.

Missing is the sober awareness of the solidarity of the human family and our corporate guilt. We're in this together! When will we wake up to this redemptive fact? The sooner we face up to our collective pride and greed and envy and anarchy, the sooner we accept our guilt as man before God, the sooner we can expect to see forgiveness and healing, renewal and peace, God's way on God's conditions.

"All we like sheep have gone astray; we have turned everyone to his own way..." (Isaiah 53:6). "If My people, which are called by My Name, will turn from their wicked ways; then will I hear from Heaven ...and heal their land" (II Chronicles 7:14).

§ FUNDAMENTALS

"*F*undamentalist!", a nasty word in some circles, nevertheless fundamentals are absolutely imperative today!

Athletes who ignore fundamentals make losing teams.

Sputnik aroused us to our neglect of fundamentals in education. We hope the awakening did not come too late.

This is precisely the point of our frustration today. We are trying to preserve Western civilization while at the same time we repudiate its basis! Struggling to patch up the superstructure, we allow the foundation to go unattended and forgotten. (Occasional termite inspections are not enough.)

We seek the benefits of Christianity, and reject the source of those benefits! Obviously, if we insist on abandoning the root of our culture, the loss of the fruit is inevitable! Our struggle is as futile as the attempt to preserve a flower that has been cut from its roots. The fragrance and beauty linger for a while, but they are temporary!

Like parasites we are feeding on lingering blessings produced by the spiritual leadership and dedication of earlier generations; the blessings are fading; ethical and moral levels decline toward an increasingly degenerate society. How do we get life and vitality, bloom and fragrance back into our culture?

Take a leaf from Israel's history. The Old Testament records her disintegration so graphically. She fought to preserve the effects of her spiritual destiny, but she rejected God! Her religion grew sterile and stagnant, a "form of Godliness, denying the power." She worshiped God with her lips; her heart was far from Him!

This is fundamental! Man alienated from God by sin. God sent His Son into history to reconcile man to Himself. Christ died on the cross for man's sin; rose from the dead for man's justification. This is fundamental to Christianity; fundamental to our society!

Regenerate man, trusting in Christ as Savior, obeying Christ as Lord, is the key to healthy, free, vigorous society. God demands more than patrons; He will be served! Christ wants more than admirers; He seeks disciples!

Let America repent! Let repentance begin with you! Let us pray for genuine spiritual awakening! Let it begin with you!

"Seek ye first the Kingdom of God, and His righteousness..." (Matthew 6:33).

§ BEAUTY? ARTIFICIAL OR REAL?

*C*onsider the Christmas tree: millions of homes will be graced with its beauty, millions of families gather about its festooned branches, millions of children are filled with gaiety and excitement by its brilliance. But within two weeks it will be relegated to the trash can; from beauty to ashes, from happy fireside to garbage truck, so it goes.

Because the Christmas tree is lifeless! Too soon its needles fall leaving bare, unattractive branches. Most of its beauty consisted in what the family put on it; tinsel, bright ornaments, colored lights, artificial snow; maybe expensive, maybe cheap; some gaudy, some conservative, but all on the outside of the tree, temporary, removable.

How different the tree in the forest! Its needles remain permanently green and fresh, giving refreshing shade in the heat of the day, luxurious beauty to the landscape, and it is cherished for generations. Because it is planted, it has life within! Its beauty is not artificial; it is the authentic beauty flowing from inner life, health, and strength.

Men are like trees! The only beauty some have is what they wear; clothing and jewelry, superficial culture and surface morality; it may be gaudy and colorful, conservative and plain. Whatever its form, the value of the man is what he puts on like a garment. It is artificial, temporary, unreal, and deterioration is inevitable.

Men like this are attractive, just like the Christmas tree, but glitter doesn't last, lights burn out, colors fade, culture wears thin, and folks soon lose interest. Oh the inconceivable loneliness of the man whose beauty is purchased and put on, whose attraction is external and transitory.

What contrast the man who has the eternal life of God within; whose beauty cannot wither or fade, whose Christ-like fragrance is perennial, whose attraction is deathless.

"Blessed is the man that walketh not in the counsel of the ungodly, nor standeth in the way of sinners, nor sitteth in the seat of the scornful. But his delight is in the law of the Lord; and in His law doth he meditate day and night. And he shall be like a tree planted by the rivers of water, that bringeth forth his fruit in his season; his leaf also shall not wither; and whatsoever he doeth shall prosper" (Psalm 1:1-3).

§ THE LEGACY OF CHRISTMAS

*O*ne great dominant conviction emerges as the nostaligic promise of Christmas reflects against the backdrop of convulsive human affairs; God's eternal gift was not just the birth of a Babe in Bethlehem! It was that, but infinitely more; the birth of the Babe was only the beginning.

God's incalculable gift to man included the faultless life of that Babe grown to Manhood; His costly sacrifice on the cross of Calvary; His mighty Resurrection from the grave; and the absolute certainty of His return in triumph to reign forever, King of kings and Lord of lords! In the words of one eminent contemporary Christian, "Jesus Christ, the Word of God Incarnate, shall triumph in history, and not merely beyond history" (John A. Mackay).

Jesus Christ *is* Lord of all! This deep, solid, stubborn conviction is at the very heart of the New Testament, and it is implicit in all of the Old Testament and gloriously explicit in many of the Old Testament prophets.

Jesus Christ, the Word of God Incarnate, is the Lord of history; He is the Lord of the universe! And the plain, irresistible fact is that all humanity and all the universe find their true satisfaction in consent and obedience to His Lordship. The deepest longings and aspirations of humanity are to be fulfilled when Jesus Christ returns to claim His universal, eternal crown! Hence the relevance of the glorious legacy of Christmas: "Glory to God in the highest, and on earth, peace among men of good will." Not unqualified peace, but peace among men whose wills are right; right with the Lord of Heaven and earth and therefore right with each other.

"Fear not: for, behold, I bring you good tidings of great joy, which shall be to all people. For unto you is born this day in the city of David a Savior, which is Christ the Lord" (Luke 2:10-11).

"*N*o vacancy!" Familiar words! But have you ever stopped to think of the misery, the desperation they bring into lives? Who can measure the frustration, despair, defeat for those shut out by this hard, unfeeling voice? "No vacancy!" Discouragement, heartbreak, tragedy.

In the dead of the night, along some highway, the screech of brakes, grinding of metal, hollow tinkling of glass, sickening thud of bodies, then silence! The unearthly silence of injured and dying. Someone driving through the night. Motel after motel carried the "no vacancy" sign. On they drive, hoping against hope, until sleep wins out, and death! Volumes could be filled with the pathetic tragedies of smashed lives, the ruin wrought by "no vacancy"!

But the saddest time in history was the night when these words shut out the Son of God. Just a brief unfeeling phrase in the record, "There was no room in the inn." It is a stinging, scathing, damning rebuke to the world! What an indictment, no room for Him! for Christ! It is incredible, but true. What a reception for the Son of God, the Prince of Peace. Is it any wonder peace is so elusive when we reject the only One who can bring it?

Nineteen wide centuries have passed. The sign is still out! It still hangs over many hearts, many homes, many offices. "No vacancy!" For Christ! He has been crowded out by the traffic, the congestion, the cold, hard materialism of our secular lives. He's just an X now, the unknown in Xmas.

There is a difference when there is room for Him in the life! Christmas is more than a holiday then; it is a holy day too. He brings peace, joy, comfort, stability, strength, hope when we let Him in. Have you ever really made room for Him? Be honest with yourself if with no other! Have you allowed this matchless Son of God to be crowded out of your life? Are you too busy for Him? Then you are too busy! This is Christmas in essence: God coming into the world in the Person of Christ. This is its application: Christ coming into your life dispelling sin, dispeace, despair, with His peerless Presence.

"Behold I [Christ] stand at the door [of your heart] and knock; if any man hear My voice, and open the door, I will come in..." (Revelation 3:20).

§ *CHRISTMAS IS TO RECEIVE*

*T*here are two sides to a gift, giving and receiving! Both are required to complete a gift.

Nothing is more humiliating to the giver than to have his gift ignored or refused. Nothing is more insulting to a giver than rejection! He cannot force the gift; he can only offer it.

"God so loved—that He gave...." This is the point of Christmas, the heart of Christianity, the heart of the Hebrew-Christian, the Bible record! A loving God, a giving God!

This love of God's, this gift of God's, distinguishes Christianity from all other religions. God gave, man is intended to receive! Reduced to its simplest terms, the message of the Bible is this loving and giving of God to man, and the supreme tragedy in the Biblical record is man's perennial failure to receive this love, this gift. This in fact is the very root of the human dilemma!

Christmas means comparatively little more than a headache, extra bills and exhaustion to the man who has not responded to God's love and received His gift because Christmas is incomplete, only half a transaction.

The coming of the Son of God into history by way of the virgin birth was meant to be more than an historical act; it was meant to be a personal experience for man. Jesus came into history that He might enter man's heart and abide there.

Is Christmas a personal experience for you or simply a perfunctory celebration of an event 1900 years old which has no relevance for your life? If Christmas is impersonal to you, receive God's gift now; let this be the most significant Christmas of your life; let God's Son be born in your heart.

"But as many as received Him, to them gave He power to become the sons of God..." (John 1:12).

§ OVERCOME EVIL

*T*here is nothing complicated about the mathematics of the spirit. Actually it is just as simple, as logical, as two plus two, and just as irrevocable. Once a man has learned this simple arithmetic and its application to the spiritual and moral realm, he is a long way toward maturity. He is on the road to being an adult.

Take an example: Two wrongs do not make a right. That is obvious to the most shallow thinker. Adding wrong to wrong cannot by the cleverest manipulation be made to come out right. Two wrongs add up to *twice as much* wrong. Add evil to evil, the result is twice as much evil. That is plain horse-sense. And it works out that way in real life, with the result that many men mess up their lives continually because they forget spiritual math, or try to manipulate it, or ignore it. Even intelligent men.

To illustrate: A few nights ago at a busy intersection two new Cadillacs had a slight altercation. Actually it was nothing at all, but the drivers of the two cars made stupid fools of themselves. It happened this way: The first car didn't pull away from the signal as fast as the second car thought it should. Man in the second car began honking his horn; man in the first car got mad at the horn, refused to budge; man in the second car beat on his horn, blasted away. Meanwhile traffic was tied up in that lane for a block, and there sat two new Cadillacs with their drivers acting like juveniles, amidst the honking of many horns. After two or three signals the rear driver got desperate, rammed the rear of the first car.

Result: A nasty argument, loud words, cursing and name-calling, a gathering crowd, and in the big middle two nicely dressed men, intelligent looking, old enough to know better, acting like six-year-olds. What a pathetic sight! The math of the spirit. But men do it all the time; get themselves all tied up in knots over silly little things that shouldn't bother big people at all. Why don't we wise up?

It doesn't many any difference what people do to you, how evil they treat you, the *damage* isn't done until you react to it. Not how they treat you, but how you take it! Retaliate wrong for wrong, nothing's gained. You *lose*! Prestige, self-respect, and worst of all, something happens inside you that makes you less a man. This is what the Bible means when it says "Do not be *overcome* with evil, but overcome evil with good." Respond to evil with evil, one is overcome with evil; the damage is doubled, or worse. Meet evil with good; evil is canceled out. You're a better man by far. That's the mathematics of the spirit. That's intelligent, practical, effective living. That's what separates the men from the boys.

§ *LOVE IS NOT SOFT*

*H*ave you considered the intolerance of love?

Love will tolerate anything against itself, but beware of its concern for the beloved! There is a kind of tolerance abroad today which is a caricature of true love. Tolerance may indicate the absence of love! Actually it is nothing more than lack of conviction; a cover-up for indifference! "The man who stands for nothing, falls for anything!"

Love is the strongest force in the world! But let's be sure we understand love. Backbone of love is integrity and justice. Without integrity, without justice, love is sheer sentimentality. It is lazy and indulgent. It makes a mockery of true love.

Love may manifest itself in judgment!

Jesus never defended Himself, but in love for God He drove from the temple the moneychangers who had commercialized religion. He was the most magnanimous Man who ever lived, but His righteous indignation flashed fire at the hypocrite and the phony.

It is one thing to defend one's self; quite another to defend a principle or a loved one. Love will not tolerate that which threatens the beloved, even when that threat resides within the beloved himself. Love reserves the right to be critical of the beloved, to discipline, to frustrate. It does not over-protect or smother or possess. It does not play at being an amateur providence in other lives. Love often leaves alone!

Love burns with intolerance for dishonesty; hypocrisy; selfishness; greed; covetousness; evil jealousy; pride. Love is sacrificial.

Gives itself away; denies itself; dies to itself! Love always pays a price. *Love is costly.*

True love is not generated by man; it originates with God, but will be reflected in the man who walks with God! Cure for lovelessness is surrender to Christ!

"God so loved the world, that He gave His only begotten Son..." (John 3:16).

"Herein is love, not that we loved God, but that He loved us, and sent His Son to be the propitiation [substitute] for our sins. Beloved, if God so loved us, we ought also to love one another" (I John 4:10, 11).

§ *GOD'S LOVE DOES NOT EXCLUDE SUFFERING*

"*H*ow can you believe in a God of love when there is so much suffering in the world?" That question was addressed violently to a pastor as he sat in a wheelchair in the patio of a hospital recuperating from a siege of illness. The speaker was a woman, also in a wheelchair, who had undergone much suffering.

"Do you believe in suffering?" asked the pastor. "What do you mean by that?" the woman replied. "Is suffering real?" continued the man; "Is suffering a fact?"

"Is it a fact!" she exclaimed bitterly. "You don't spend three weeks in a hospital listening to the screams of women and children; seeing a woman brought into your ward one day, carried out under a sheet the next; you don't stay in the hospital as I have these last three weeks and have any doubt that suffering is real. Of course suffering is a fact!" For thirty minutes the woman poured out the bitterness and cynicism that had soured in her soul as she suffered through her days in a hospital bed.

"Very well, suffering is a fact. On this we agree," said the pastor. "Now how do you explain this suffering without a belief in a God of love? Does suffering make any more sense without a belief in a God of love? Is suffering more bearable when you don't believe in a God of love?"

The woman was quiet for a long time as it slowly dawned on her that consciously or unconsciously the only thing that kept her sane through her intense suffering was the feeling that somehow, somewhere there was a God who cared, who loved, who understood. Overcome by self-pity she allowed bitterness to distort her reason, to make her angry with God, and to fight back by trying to deny Him.

It may be difficult to explain how a God of love could allow the terrible agony and suffering and tragedy in the world, but it is infinitely more difficult to explain these facts of life, and leave God out of the picture! Life is certainly a "tale told by an idiot, full of sound and fury, signifying nothing..." if a loving God is nonexistent. The suffering and tragedy remain; but there is no hope, no reason, no sense to life if man cannot count on a God who can somehow use the suffering and in His providence turn tragedy into triumph.

"We know that in everything God works for good with those who love Him, who are called according to His purpose" (Romans 8:28 [RSV]).

§ *CHRISTMAS CARRYOVER*

*T*here is supreme reassurance in Christmas as a man faces a new year!

Christmas commemorates an event, the greatest event in history. This reminds us that Christian hope rests, not in ideas nor ethics nor theology, but in objective events in history. This is the thing that validates Christian faith: *It is founded upon solid fact*, not theory nor speculation. There are many qualities about this *fact* of Christmas that set it apart from all other historical events. The birth of Christ was unique in history. Nothing else like it ever happened!

It was unique in its anticipation. Hundreds of years before it happened there were scores of specific predictions concerning it: How He would be born. Where He would be born. His Name, etc. It is mathematically impossible for these specific predictions to be coincidental. *Their fulfillment testifies irrefutably* to this event *as Divine*! It was unique in its plan. Never before or since has a virgin conceived and borne a child. This was to be the "sign" according to Isaiah 700 years earlier. This was God's way of entering into human affairs to do for man what he could not do for himself. And it was unique in its purpose! All others are born to live. Jesus Christ was born to die! His supreme purpose in coming into the world was to lay down His life as the sacrifice for sin.

The cross was not an interruption, not an unfortunate, unexpected, undesired and premature end to an otherwise glorious life. On the contrary, the cross was the goal, the objective, the realization of God's purpose in history. He came to die on a cross! The "Lamb of God that taketh away sin...." Which is the reason why this event is so uniquely significant in history. Why Christmas holds such genuine reassurance in an inflammable world at the turn of the year. The birth, life, death, and Resurrection of Jesus Christ were in order to redeem man. They were God's redemptive acts within history!

There is an immediacy, a relevancy about these redemptive acts of God in Christ. They are practical. They work now, today! They make it possible for a man to begin again as though he had not had a failure or a blunder or a fault or a sin in the past. A man can start the new year with a clean slate. All the past can be under the exhaustless grace of God, covered by the sacrifice of Jesus Christ. Man's sin and error are forever forgotten by God when man turns to Christ in confession and surrender. This is the glorious, the incredible, the phenomenal fact behind the Christmas event. Jesus Christ came into the world to save sinners. And He really does. If a man will turn to Him, let Him come into his heart.

"Glory to God, peace on earth among men of *good will*...."

TOPIC INDEX